v013118
pc: 214
ISBN Printed Book: 9781944607210
ISBN eBook: 9781944607227

**Notice:** Although IconLogic makes every effort to ensure the accuracy and quality of these materials, all material is provided without any warranty.

# Abrams' Guide to Grammar
# Third Edition

"Skills and Drills" Learning

Ellie Abrams

## About The Author

**Ellie Abrams**, president of ESA Editorial and Training Services Inc., has conducted training seminars for a wide spectrum of clients. Writers, editors, secretaries, managers, administrative staff, proofreaders, lawyers, educators, scientists, and students have benefited from her expertise. Ellie co-authored *The New York Public Library Writer's Guide to Style and Usage* and *STET Again!*

*to my mother,*

*Edith W. Silverblatt,*

*who taught me that learning never stops*

"Skills and Drills" Learning

# Contents

## Module 9: Modifiers

## Supplemental Exercises

## Supplemental Exercises: Answer Key

# Notes

# Preface

If you are a "word" person—a writer, editor, or proofreader—you will get a refresher on every aspect of English grammar and increase your ability to analyze, correct, and explain grammar and punctuation problems you find in the materials you work on. If you are a student, you will get a strong foundation in the fundamentals of English grammar. If English is not your first language, you will find clear, concise information on the structure and grammar of the English language. If any of this rings true, my book can help. Each exercise offers a thorough explanation in the answer key.

To master grammar, you have to have the right tools for the job. Every profession has its tools: electricians have their wires, artists have their palettes, programmers have their computers, and surgeons have their scalpels. But we "word" people are often expected to do our jobs with no tools. In addition, most professionals do not have to share their tools, but we in the "word" world usually do.

What tools do "word" people need? Actually, there are lots of helpful tools, but three are essential.

## Tools... Tools... Tools...

First, you need an up-to-date, in-depth **grammar book**. You might find it useful to keep the following in mind: *no rule of grammar is worth memorizing, but every rule is worth looking up.* You are not a walking encyclopedia of grammar knowledge. It is not necessary to know, for instance, if a question mark goes inside or outside quotation marks. If you have a good grammar book, the answer will be easy to find. Look up "question mark," use it correctly, and be done with it. (Don't worry about memorizing rules that are in the "get-a-life" category. You can use your grammar reference book to look things up again and again. The rules that you use most often will become ingrained.) We must know what we do not know and take the time to use our resources.

Second, you need a **style manual**. Whether you use the *United States Government Printing Office Style Manual, Chicago Manual of Style, Publication Manual of the American Psychological Association, Associated Press Stylebook and Briefing on Media Law,* or your own

company style manual, the style manual is essential in resolving style issues such as spelling, capitalization, numbers, compounding, abbreviations, and optional punctuation (for example, the serial comma and apostrophes).

Third, you need a **dictionary**. Your dictionary should have a copyright date within the past five years. Our language is ever-changing; society dictates language, and language dictates society. We "word" people need to keep up with the times. Here's another important point concerning dictionaries. Does your spell check match the dictionary in your word processor? It should. Does you style manual dictate which dictionary you should be using? *Random House*? *American Heritage*? *Webster's*? Are you using an online dictionary? Is everyone on your project using the same dictionary? Is *copyediting* one word? Two words? Hyphenated? Does *dissension* end in *-tion* or *-sion*?

Checking a document for errors takes a lot of time. A document can be "slow and clean" or "quick and dirty." Although most "word" people believe in "slow and clean," many supervisors expect "quick and clean"—an unlikely pair.

This book will help "word" people, from writer to substantive editor to copyeditor to proofreader to student, produce "slow and clean" documents.

# Module 1: Parts of Speech and Parts of a Sentence

## Parts of Speech

If I were to ask you how many parts of speech we have in the language, I'm sure you would say "eight" and rattle them off: *noun, pronoun, verb, adjective, adverb, preposition, conjunction, and interjection.* So I won't ask.

Remember those horrible vocabulary assignments given to you by your seventh-grade English teacher: "Look up twenty-five words and write the definition, the part of speech, and a sentence." By the time you got to the end of the list, you were just happy to be done. You probably had no idea what any of the words meant or how they should really be used. The truth is, *no word is a part of speech until it's used in a sentence.*

I'll give you six sentences using the word *down*, and each time I use it, it will be a different part of speech.

- ❐ Eric fell *down.* (In this sentence *down* is an adverb because it modifies the verb *fell*.)

- ❐ Eric fell *down* the stairs. (In this sentence *down* is a preposition because it shows the relationship between two nouns: *Eric* and *stairs*.)

- ❐ The quilt is made of eider *down.* (In this sentence *down* is a noun because it names a thing.)

- ❐ The *down* escalator was broken. (In this sentence *down* is an adjective because it modifies a noun.)

- ❐ She *downed* the ball on the fifty-yard line. (In this sentence *down* is a verb because it is the action of the sentence.)

- ❐ *Down!* (Okay, so I cheated a bit here. In this sentence *down* is acting like an interjection, but I guess we would agree that it is really an adverb because it modifies the understood verb *get* as in "Get down!")

As a word person, you may not be asked often to label the part of speech of words, but when you are editing and proofreading, it's a good idea to have the ammunition to support your changes.

# Definitions

**Noun:** Names a person, place, or thing. A noun can be a common noun, such as *friend, monument, river,* and *street,* or a proper noun, such as *Ellen, Washington Monument, Hudson River,* and *Main Street.* A noun can name something concrete, such as a *chair, computer, dog,* or *desk,* or something abstract, such as *love, justice, honor,* or *friendship.* Possessive nouns are adjectives because they modify nouns: *Susan's* bike, *Alfonso's* idea, *Jacob's* car, and *Hasim's* music.

**Pronoun:** Takes the place of a noun. Pronouns include personal pronouns, such as *I, she, we,* and *they.* Pronouns also include words such as *this, that, these, those, who, whom, some, most, many, all.* Possessive pronouns such as *his, hers, ours,* and *mine* can stand alone (This is his). Possessive pronouns such as *his, her, our,* and *my* modify nouns and are adjectives (This book is his book).

**Adjective:** Describes a noun or a pronoun. Adjectives answer the following questions: What kind? How many? Which one? Adjectives include words such as *large, one, the, a, funny,* and *happy.*

**Verb:** Expresses an action or a state of being. Verbs include overt actions, such as *run, laugh, write,* and *sing.* Verbs also include mental actions, such as *think, decide, review,* and *love.* State of being verbs include words such as *is, are, was, will be.*

**Adverb:** Describes a verb, an adjective, or another adverb. Adverbs answer the following questions: How? Why? When? Where? To what degree? What direction? In what manner? The following words can function as adverbs: *quickly, very, quite, somewhat, intelligently, there.*

**Conjunction**: Connects two words or phrases or clauses. Conjunctions include simple coordinating conjunctions: *for, and, nor, but, or, yet.* Conjunctions also include subordinating conjunctions (*if, until, unless, when, where, because*) and correlative conjunctions (*either/or, neither/nor*).

**Preposition:** Stands before a noun or pronoun and together with that noun or pronoun becomes a phrase modifying something else in the sentence. A preposition shows the relationship between two nouns, two pronouns, or a noun and a pronoun. The following words are examples of prepositions: *in, for, to, under, around, above.*

**Interjection:** Expresses an exclamation in the middle of a sentence without grammatical connection to other words. The following words are interjections: *ouch, ah, oh, oops.* Interjections should not be used in business or academic writing.

# Confidence Check

Identify the nouns (N), the verbs (V), and the pronouns (P) in the following sentences.

1. We saw an exciting game last Tuesday.

2. The pitcher threw him a fastball.

3. She and I go every Saturday to the game at the stadium.

4. Switch-hitting Mickey Mantle was inducted into the Hall of Fame in 1974, the first year he was eligible.

5. Hurricane Katrina left New Orleans a disaster area.

6. In Katrina's aftermath, the Coast Guard rescued or evacuated more than 33,500 people.

7. The Coast Guard was saving lives before any other federal agency, even though almost half the local Coast Guard personnel lost their own homes in the hurricane.

8. Aviation-safety programs focus on the prevention of accidents and incidents.

9. The focus of the program is on safety issues during adverse weather conditions.

10. General aviation pilots must modify personal lifestyle factors because they may cause fatigue.

11. The Smithsonian, America's national education facility, consists of 19 museums, 9 research centers, and over 140 affiliate museums around the world.

12. During their senior year, students research a topic of interest to them.

13. The Census Bureau serves as the leading source of quality data about the nation's people and economy.

14. We honor privacy, protect confidentiality, share our expertise globally, and conduct our work openly.

15. The association provides business management articles, webcasts, online learning, and books to anyone who purchases a one-year membership.

16. She liked geography, hated home economics, and tolerated algebra, but she adored history.

17. An estimated 190 million acres of federal forests and rangelands in the United States face high risk of catastrophic fires.

18. These fires could severely impact people, communities, and natural resources.

19. We manage a variety of water and underwater resources, including 472 dams and 348 reservoirs.

20. The U.S. Geological Survey scientists monitor and assess water quality, streamflows, and ground water at thousands of sites across the nation.

# Confidence Check Answers

1. We (P), saw (V), game (N), Tuesday (N)

2. pitcher (N),  threw (V), him (P), fastball (N)

3. She (P), I (P), go (V), Saturday (N), game (N), stadium (N)

4. Mickey Mantle (N), was inducted (V), Hall of Fame (N), 1974 (N), year (N ), he (P), was (V)

5. Hurricane Katrina (N ), left (V), New Orleans (N), area (N) (some dictionaries may have "disaster area" as a two-word noun)

6. aftermath (N), Coast Guard (N ), rescued (V), evacuated (V), more (P), people (N)

7. Coast Guard (N ), was saving (V), lives (N), agency (N), half (N), personnel (N), lost (V), homes (N), hurricane (N)

8. programs (N), focus (V), prevention (N), accidents (N), incidents (N)

9. focus (N), is (V), issues (N), conditions (N), program (N)

10. pilots (N), must modify (V), factors (N), they (P), may cause (V), fatigue (N)

11. Smithsonian (N), facility (N ), consists (V), museums (N), centers (N), museums (N), world (N)

12. year (N), students (N), research (V), topic (N), interest (N), them (P)

13. Census Bureau (N), serves (V), source (N ), data (N), people (N), economy (N)

14. We (P), honor (V), privacy (N), protect (V ), confidentiality (N), share (V), expertise (N), conduct (V), work (N)

15. association (N), provides (V), articles (N), webcasts (N), learning (N), books (N), anyone (P), who (P), purchases (V), membership (N)

16. She (P), liked (V), geography (N), hated (V),  home economics (N), tolerated (V), algebra (N), she (P ), adored (V ), history (N)

17. acres (N), forests (N), rangelands (N), United States (N ), face (V), risk (N), fires (N)

18. fires (N), could impact (V), people (N), communities (N), resources (N)

19. We (P), manage (V), variety (N), resources (N), dams (N), reservoirs (N)

20. scientists (N ), monitor (V), assess (V), quality (N), streamflows (N), water (N), thousands (N), sites (N), nation (N) (Some dictionaries may list *groundwater* as one word.)

# Confidence Check

Identify the part of speech of each italicized word as a noun (N), pronoun (P), verb (V), adjective (Adj), adverb (Adv), or preposition (Prep).

1. Most of the *other* accountants consider Newman *reliable.*

2. Too much *reliance* on *others* can stifle a person's independence.

3. The company president *relied* on the new marketing director to increase sales *considerably.*

4. The young hikers *climbed up* the steep, slippery slope.

5. Sit *down*, Melissa, and please speak *quietly.*

6. *Your* coffee mug is here; *theirs* are on the counter.

7. Of the three CD players, the *portable* one works *best.*

8. We get the *best* sound *from* the portable CD player.

9. This fifth draft *finally satisfied* the chairperson.

10. Because I had not studied adequately, I performed *unsatisfactorily* on the *final* examination.

11. *After* the rehearsal, the choir sang *better.*

12. A *better choice* might be the less expensive one.

13. A *friendly* airline employee led *us* to the correct terminal.

14. *One* of the scout leaders *befriended* the shy newcomer.

15. *One* survivor of the earthquake sought *refuge* in an abandoned warehouse.

16. Aunt Martha *still* exhibits a *youthful* appearance.

17. *Nobody* ranked *above* us in the science fair.

18. High *above*, an eagle soared *majestically.*

19. *That* was a *most* important observation.

20. *That* law affects *most* public schools.

21. *Neither* of his two new novels was *popular* with his fans.

22. *Neither* novel gained the *popularity* he had hoped for.

23. Your *behavior* at the family reunion was *deplorable.*

24. She *behaved deplorably* at the family reunion.

25. *Several* of the skiers ventured *beyond* the safety fence.

26. *Several* skiers returned *safely* to the lodge after dark.

27. *Who* felt *bad* about the situation?

28. She *felt* the different yarns *carefully* before she purchased the mohair.

# Confidence Check Answers

1. other (ADJ), reliable (ADJ)

2. reliance (N), others (P)

3. relied (V), considerably (ADV)

4. climbed (V), up (Prep)

5. down (ADV), quietly (ADV)

6. Your (ADJ), theirs (P)

7. portable (ADJ), best (ADV)

8. best (ADJ), from (Prep)

9. finally (ADV), satisfied (V)

10. unsatisfactorily (ADV), final (ADJ)

11. After (Prep), better (ADV)

12. better (ADJ), choice (N)

13. friendly (ADJ), us (P)

14. One (P), befriended (V)

15. One (ADJ), refuge (N),

16. still (ADV), youthful (ADJ)

17. Nobody (P), above (Prep)

18. above (ADV), majestically (ADV)

19. That (P), most (ADV)

20. That (ADJ), most (ADJ)

21. Neither (P), popular (ADJ)

22. Neither (ADJ), popularity (N)

23. behavior (N), deplorable (ADJ)

24. behaved (V), deplorably (ADV)

25. Several (P), beyond (Prep)

26. Several (ADJ), safely (ADV)

27. Who (P), bad (ADJ)

28. felt (V), carefully (ADV)

# Basic Patterns

A sentence is made of two basic parts: the subject and the predicate. When you are writing and editing, you may not have to identify the parts of a sentence, but knowing the five basic sentence patterns can be helpful. The following chart gives you the basic sentence patterns with examples. Subjects of a sentence can be single words, phrases, or clauses (we will discuss phrases and clauses in a later module). The predicate always includes a verb and may include a direct object, a subject complement (it "completes" the subject and is often called either a predicate noun (nominative) or a predicate adjective, an indirect object, and/or an object complement (it "completes" a direct or indirect object). Both the subject and the verb can contain modifying words, phrases, and clauses.

| Five Basic Sentence Patterns | | | |
|---|---|---|---|
| **Subject** | **Predicate** | | |
| **Subject** | **Verb** | | |
| The plane | landed. | | |
| Interest rates | have dropped. | | |
| **Subject** | **Verb** | **Direct Object** | |
| The hurricane | flooded | the city. | |
| Giant pandas | eat | bamboo. | |
| **Subject** | **Verb** | **Subject Complement** | |
| Knowledge | is | power. (predicate noun) | |
| Lemmings | are | intriguing. (predicate adjective) | |
| **Subject** | **Verb** | **Indirect Object** | **Direct Object** |
| The manager | offered | Louise | the baseball tickets. |
| The golf pro | gives | my brother | a weekly lesson. |
| **Subject** | **Verb** | **Direct Object** | **Object Complement** |
| The contractor | painted | the house | green. (adjective) |
| The governor | declared | the county | a disaster area. (noun) |

# Notes

# Module 2: Clauses and Phrases

## Clauses

### Independent Clauses

A sentence needs a subject and a verb. It must include at least one clause capable of standing alone (independent clause). An **independent clause** contains a subject and a verb and makes a complete statement.

### Dependent Clauses

A **dependent clause** may not stand alone as a sentence. Although it contains both a subject and a verb, a dependent clause does not express a complete statement. A dependent clause can be one of three types: (1) subordinate, (2) relative, or (3) noun.

### 1. Subordinate Clauses

Subordinate clauses begin with subordinating conjunctions and function as adverbs (they are also called adverbial clauses). The following words (subordinating conjunctions), and other similar words, make a clause incapable of standing alone.

| | |
|---|---|
| after | if |
| although | when |
| as | since |
| as if | whenever |
| as though | though |
| before | unless |
| because | until |

❏ She acts *as if she knows the subject quite well*.

❏ Many magazines in the 1800s had no photographs *when they were first published*.

❏ *Unless we hire an additional editor*, we will not meet our deadline.

## 2. Relative Clauses

Relative clauses begin with *that, which, where, who, whom,* or *whose* and function as adjectives (they are also called adjective clauses).

❏ I will never forget the day *that I graduated*.

❏ The building *where I work* is being renovated.

❏ The woman *whose sister won the lottery* is excited.

❏ Students *who sit in the front row* usually participate more than other students.

## 3. Noun Clauses

Noun clauses perform the same functions in sentences that nouns do.

A noun clause can be a **subject of a verb**:

❏ *What Fred said* shocked his friends.

A noun clause can be a **direct object**:

❏ Denise's friends did not know *that she could not swim*.

A noun clause can be a **subject complement (predicate nominative)**:

❏ Penny's mistake was *that she refused to listen to good advice*.

A noun clause can be an **object of a preposition**:

❏ Jessica is not responsible for *what Rhodes did*.

# Confidence Check

Identify all the independent and dependent clauses in the following sentences. Mark each dependent clause as subordinate (adverbial), relative (adjective), or noun.

1. Her most recent book, which made our book club list, is not in any local book stores.

2. While Juan was preparing his presentation, he worried about the time limit.

3. Have you considered hiring Kim, who received several awards for excellence in design last year?

4. Kelsey wants to visit her family in Australia before she starts her new job and after she tours New Zealand.

5. Frank always visits his sister, but she never comes to see him. (This sentence has no dependent clauses. It is composed of two independent clauses joined by a coordinating conjunction.)

6. Whoever broke the vase will pay for it before we order a new one.

7. Some firefighters never meet the people whom they save.

8. Barbara was annoyed by what the professor asked her.

9. After Eva and Ethan left on the bus, they realized that Jim was waiting at the train station.

10. When the team won the championship, the coach hugged his players, and the fans cheered.

# Confidence Check Answers

Independent clauses are in plain text; dependent clauses are in italics with an explanation in parentheses.

1. Her most recent book, *which made our book club list,* is not in any local book stores. (The dependent clause *which made our book club list* is a relative clause modifying the noun *book.*)

2. *While Juan was preparing his presentation,* he worried about the time limit. (The dependent clause *While Juan was preparing his presentation* is a subordinate clause modifying the verb *worried.*)

3. Have you considered hiring Kim, *who received several awards for excellence in design last year*? (The dependent clause *who received several awards for excellence in design last year* is a relative clause modifying the noun *Kim.*)

4. Kelsey wants to visit her family in Australia *before she starts her new job* and *after she tours New Zealand*. (The dependent clauses *before she starts her new job* and *after she tours New Zealand* are subordinate clauses modifying the verb *visit.*)

5. Frank always visits his sister, but she never comes to see him.

6. *Whoever broke the vase* will pay for it *before we order a new one*. (The dependent clause *Whoever broke the vase* is a noun clause because it is the subject of the sentence; the dependent clause *before we order a new one* is a subordinate clause modifying the verb *pay.*)

7. Some firefighters never meet the people *whom they save*. (The dependent clause *whom they save* is a relative clause modifying the noun *people.*)

8. Barbara was annoyed by *what the professor asked her*. (The dependent clause *what the professor asked her* is a noun clause functioning as the object of the preposition *by.*)

9. *After Eva and Ethan left on the bus*, they realized *that Jim was waiting at the train station*. (The dependent clause *After Eva and Ethan left on the bus*, is a subordinate clause modifying the verb *realized*; the dependent clause *that Jim was waiting at the train station* is a noun clause functioning as a direct object.)

10. *When the team won the championship*, the coach hugged his players, and the fans cheered. (The dependent clause *When the team won the championship* is a subordinate clause modifying the verbs *hugged* and *cheered.*)

# Prepositional Phrases

A preposition shows the relationship between a noun or a pronoun and some other word in the sentence. A prepositional phrase is made up of a preposition and its object (a noun, a pronoun, a gerund or gerund phrase, or a noun clause) and any associated adjectives or adverbs. A prepositional phrase can function as a noun, an adjective, or an adverb. Usually, prepositions are used to show where something is located or when something happened.

Here are some common prepositions.

| | | | | | |
|---|---|---|---|---|---|
| about | at | despite | in place of | out | unlike |
| above | because of | down | inside | out of | until |
| according to | before | during | in spite of | outside | up |
| across | behind | except | instead of | over | upon |
| after | below | except for | into | past | up to |
| against | beneath | excepting | like | regarding | via |
| along | beside | for | near | than | while |
| along with | between | from | next | through | with |
| among | beyond | in | of | throughout | within |
| apart from | but | in addition to | off | to | without |
| around | by | in back of | on | toward | |
| as | by means of | in case of | onto | under | |
| as for | concerning | in front of | on top of | underneath | |

❑ *Out of sight* is *out of mind*. (Both preposition phrases function as nouns. The phrase *out of sight* is the subject of the sentence; the phrase *out of mind* is a predicate nominative.)

❑ *After what they had done*, they expected a raise. (The prepositional phrase *after what they had done* is made up of the preposition *after* and the noun clause *what they had done*. The phrase is an adverbial phrase because it modifies the verb *expected*.)

❑ The representative *of our district* voted *against the referendum*. (The phrase *of our district* is an adjectival phrase because it modifies the noun *representative*; the phrase *against the referendum* is an adverbial phrase because it modifies the verb *voted*.)

❑ *Because of the inclement weather*, I cancelled my trip *to the beach*. (The prepositional phrase b*ecause of the inclement weather* is adverbial because it modifies the verb *cancelled*; the phrase *to the beach* is adjectival because it modifies the noun *trip*.)

# Confidence Check

Underline the prepositional phrases in the following sentences. Identify each as a noun, adverbial, or adjectival phrase. Indicate the way the noun phrase functions and the word the adverbial or adjectival phrase modifies.

1. With a gleam in his eye, Guinness snatched the pork chop from the dinner table.

2. That picture above the fireplace hung in my office until yesterday.

3. The articles in that journal were translated by a linguist from the university.

4. Something in the corner of the room was moving toward me.

5. After reading the manual, I understood the basics of the new software.

6. The best time to practice water conservation is before a water shortage.

7. He dreamt all his life about playing for a major league team.

8. She walked across the street, over the foot bridge, down the ramp, around the corner, and into the building.

9. Because of what the director indicated, we proofread the proposal for misspelled names.

10. From what I understand, the increase in cost resulted from mismanagement of funds.

# Confidence Check Answers

The prepositional phrases are italicized. Slashes separate phrases that are next to each other.)

1. *With a gleam / in his eye*, Guinness snatched the pork chop *from the dinner table*. (The first and third phrases are adverbial phrase because they modify the verb *snatched; the second phrase is adjectival because it modifies the noun gleam.*)

2. That picture *above the fireplace* hung *in my office / until yesterday*. (The first phrase is adjectival because it modifies the noun *picture*; the next two phrases are adverbial because they modify the verb *hung*.)

3. The articles *in that journal* were translated *by a linguist / from the university*. (The first phrase is adjectival because it modifies the noun *articles*; the next phrase is adverbial because it modifies the verb *were translated*; the last phrase is adjectival because it modifies the noun *linguist*.)

4. Something *in the corner / of the room* was moving *toward me*. (The first phrase is adjectival because it modifies the pronoun *something*; the next phrase is also adjectival because it modifies the noun *corner;* the last phrase is adverbial because it modifies the verb *was moving*.)

5. *After reading the manual*, I understood the basics *of the new software*. (The first phrase is adverbial because it modifies the verb *understood*; the next phrase is adjectival because it modifies the noun *basics*.)

6. The best time to practice water conservation is *before a water shortage*. (The phrase is a noun phrase because it is functioning as a predicate nominative.)

7. He dreamt all his life *about playing / for a major league team*. (The first phrase is adverbial because it modifies the verb *dreamt*; the next phrase is also adverbial because it modifies the gerund *playing*. Note: Although gerunds function as nouns, their modifiers are adverbs because gerunds are verbals and, therefore, have characteristics of verbs.)

8. She walked *across the street, / over the foot bridge, / down the ramp, / around the corner,* and *into the building.* (All five phrases are adverbial because they modify the verb *walked.*)

9. *Because of what the director indicated*, we proofread the proposal *for misspelled names*. (Both phrases are adverbial because they modify the verb *proofread.*)

10. *From what I understand*, the increase *in cost* resulted *from mismanagement / of funds*. (The first two phrases are adjectival because they modify the noun *increase*; the next phrase is adverbial because it modifies the verb *resulted;* the last phrase is adjectival because it modifies the noun *mismanagement*.)

# Verbals

I used to plunge into teaching the concept of parallelism without addressing the issue of verbals. But when seminar participants began stopping me in my tracks when I explained that an infinitive is not parallel with a gerund even if both terms have the same grammatical function in a sentence, I decided to revamp my approach. Realistically, you may never have to identify an infinitive, a participle, or a gerund, but you may have to verify a change you make in a document. So here's a quick look at verbals.

Verbals are words that are derived from verbs but function as other parts of speech. We have three types of verbals in our language: participles, infinitives, and gerunds.

| Type of Verbal | Part of Speech | Form of Verbal |
|---|---|---|
| participle | adjective | ends in –*ing* in the present (walking, beginning) and in –*ed* or an irregular ending in the past participle (walked, begun) |
| infinitive | noun, adjective, or adverb | the word *to* precedes the dictionary form (to walk, to begin) |
| gerund | noun | ends in an –*ing* (walking, beginning) |

Because both participles and gerunds can end in –*ing*, you have to know whether the verbal is functioning as a noun or as an adjective.

## Examples of Verbals

❏ Her **shopping** spree got her in serious financial trouble. (*Shopping* is a participle because it is functioning as an adjective modifying the noun *spree*.)

❏ **Shopping** is Samantha's favorite pastime. (*Shopping* is a gerund because it is functioning as the subject of the sentence; therefore, it is a noun.)

❏ Samantha loves **to shop**. (*To shop* is an infinitive because the verb *shop* is preceded by the word *to*. The infinitive is functioning as a direct object; therefore, it is a noun.)

# Confidence Check

Underline the verbals in the following sentences. Then identify each verbal as a participle, a gerund, or an infinitive.

1. Smoking is an addictive habit.

2. To exit, use the side entrance.

3. The dancing bear fascinated the children.

4. Seeing is believing.

5. The part to repair the broken escalator will not be available for two weeks.

6. The convertible is the one to buy.

7. Please go back to the beginning.

8. The hiking trip was the highlight of his summer vacation.

# Confidence Check Answers

1. *Smoking* is an addictive habit. (Gerund—*Smoking* is a noun functioning as the subject of the sentence.)

2. *To exit*, use the side entrance. (Infinitive—*To exit* is an infinitive functioning as an adverb that modifies the verb *use*.)

3. The *dancing* bear fascinated the children. (Participle—*Dancing* is a present participle functioning as an adjective that modifies the noun *bear*.)

4. *Seeing* is *believing*. (Gerunds—Both *seeing* and *believing* are nouns. *Seeing* is the subject of the sentence and *believing* is the predicate nominative.)

5. The part *to repair* the *broken* escalator will not be available for two weeks. (Participle—*Broken* is a past participle functioning as an adjective that modifies the noun *escalator*; *to repair* is an infinitive acting as an adjective identifying the part.)

6. The convertible is the one *to buy*. (Infinitive—*To buy* is an infinitive functioning as an adjective that modifies the pronoun *one*.)

7. Please go back to the *beginning*. (Gerund—*Beginning* is a noun functioning as the object of the preposition *to*.)

8. The *hiking* trip was the highlight of his summer vacation. (Participle—*Hiking* is a present participle functioning as an adjective that modifies the noun *trip*.)

# Verbal Phrases

A verbal phrase consists of a verbal and all of its modifiers and objects. Because verbals come from verbs, they take on all of the characteristics of verbs. And because verbals function as other parts of speech, they also take on the characteristics of those parts of speech.

- ❒ **Shopping at her favorite stores**, Samantha spent her entire paycheck. (The bolded phrase is a participial phrase because it functions as an adjective modifying *Samantha*.)

- ❒ **Shopping on line** is Samantha's favorite pastime. (The bolded phrase is a gerund phrase because it functions as the subject of the sentence; it is, therefore, a noun.)

- ❒ Samantha loves **to shop for bargains**. (The bolded phrase is an infinitive phrase because the word *to* precedes the verb. The infinitive is functioning as a direct object.)

# Confidence Check

Underline the verbal phrases in the following sentences. Then identify each verbal phrase as a participial phrase, a gerund phrase, or an infinitive phrase.

1. Skiing in Vermont is my idea of relaxation.

2. Skiing down the icy slope, I fell and broke my leg.

3. To ski every winter in Colorado will get very expensive.

4. Having been chosen for the lead role, she suddenly developed severe stage fright.

5. Lending money to a friend is a sure way to end a friendship.

6. Knowing how to access the Internet for information is a valuable skill.

7. He likes to ice skate with his partner at an ice dance competition, but his true love is to compete on the ice with his hockey team.

8. Convinced that he could win the election, he hired a campaign manager.

# Confidence Check Answers

1. *Skiing in Vermont* is my idea of relaxation. (Gerund phrase—*Skiing in Vermont* is the subject of the sentence.)

2. *Skiing down the icy slope*, I fell and broke my leg. (Participial phrase—*Skiing down the icy slope* is a present participial phrase that modifies the pronoun *I*.)

3. *To ski every winter in Colorado* will get very expensive. (Infinitive phrase—*To ski every winter in Colorado* is a noun phrase functioning as the subject of the sentence.)

4. *Having been chosen for the lead role*, she suddenly developed severe stage fright. (Participial phrase—*Having been chosen for the lead role* is a present participial phrase that modifies the pronoun *she*.)

5. *Lending money to a friend* is a sure way *to end a friendship*. (Gerund phrase— *Lending money to a friend* is the subject of the sentence. Infinitive phrase—to end a friendship is an adjective phrase modifying the noun *way*.)

6. *Knowing how to access the Internet for information* is a valuable skill. (Gerund phrase—*Knowing how to access the Internet for information* is the subject of the sentence. Infinitive phrase—Within the gerund phrase is the infinitive phrase *to access the Internet for information*.)

7. He likes *to ice skate with his partner at an ice dance competition*, but his true love is *to compete on the ice with his hockey team*. (Infinitive phrases—*to ice skate with his partner at an ice dance competition* and *to compete on the ice with his hockey team* are both noun phrases. The first one is a direct object of the verb *likes*, and the second one is a predicate nominative.)

8. *Convinced that he could win the election*, he hired a campaign manager. (Participial phrase—*Convinced that he could win the election* is a past participial phrase that modifies the pronoun *he*.)

# Sentence Fragments

A **sentence fragment** is a word group that cannot stand alone as a sentence but is punctuated as if it were a sentence. A fragment is difficult for a reader to understand because it is an incomplete statement.

Here are some examples of sentence fragments:

- ❏ Running for the bus that was turning the corner.
- ❏ The man with the large, black briefcase.
- ❏ While we waited during the rainstorm.
- ❏ In the afternoon before the meeting.
- ❏ That we had a good idea for the convention that was to be held in Houston, Texas, next month.

# Confidence Check

Identify each word group as either a sentence (S) or a fragment (F).

1. He went to the conference.

2. When he went to the conference.

3. When he went to the conference, he met with training officers from many government agencies.

4. As mentioned in the preceding letter.

5. As mentioned in the preceding letter, we will send you a draft of this year's report.

6. We will send you a draft of this year's report, although we expect many more changes.

7. Because the medical school student who graduated first in her class was serving her residency at the overcrowded hospital in her home town.

8. The medical school student who graduated first in her class was serving her residency at the overcrowded hospital in her home town.

9. We read with interest your letter of April 15 about the recent revisions to the Federal Tax Code and their implications for the U.S. economy.

10. With respect to your letter of April 15 about the recent revisions to the Federal Tax Code and their implications for the U.S. economy.

# Confidence Check Answers

1. **S**-The sentence has one independent clause.

2. **F**-The word *when* makes this word group a dependent clause.

3. **S**-The sentence has one independent clause (*he met with training officers from many government agencies*) and one dependent clause (*When he went to the conference*).

4. **F**-This word group is a phrase, because it has neither a subject nor a verb.

5. **S**-The sentence has one independent clause (*we will send you a draft of this year's report*) with an introductory phrase (*As mentioned in the preceding letter*).

6. **S**-The sentence has one independent clause (*We will send you a draft of this year's report*) and one dependent clause (*although we expect many more changes*).

7. **F**-This word group has two dependent clauses (*Because the medical school student was serving her residency at the overcrowded hospital in her home town* and *who graduated first in her class*).

8. **S**-The sentence has one independent clause (*The medical school student was serving her residency at the overcrowded hospital in her home town*) and one dependent clause (*who graduated first in her class*).

9. **S**-The sentence has one independent clause.

10. **F**-This word group is a phrase because it has neither a subject nor a verb.

# Correcting Sentence Fragments

You can take two approaches to correcting sentence fragments:

1. Combine the fragment with a related independent clause.

   ❐ Example: *We agree with your goals. Although we do not agree with your methods. (The second word group is a fragment.)*

   ❐ Possible Revision 1: *We agree with your goals, although we do not agree with your methods.*

   ❐ Possible Revision 2: *Although we do not agree with your methods, we agree with your goals.*

2. Rewrite the fragment so that it contains an independent clause.

   ❐ Revision: *We agree with your goals. We do not, however, agree with your methods.*

# Confidence Check

Correct the following fragments.

1. We would be glad to help you solve the problem. If you would send us a letter describing your current accounting procedures.

2. In response to your letter of May 6 concerning our hiring policies.

3. The report, which was completed by the April 15 deadline only through the hard work and long hours of the entire staff.

4. The approach that was recommended by the consultants whom we had contracted to solve the problem. In this approach, we increase the formal training of our analysts and hire an additional analyst.

5. After we studied the technical aspects of the proposal and our contracts office reviewed its financial aspects. The proposal, although innovative, does not meet our immediate needs.

# Possible Confidence Check Answers

1. The first word group in this example is a complete sentence; however, the second is a dependent clause because of the introductory word *if*. A dependent clause cannot stand alone. One solution could be to combine the two sentences. *We would be glad to help you solve the problem if you would send us a letter describing your current accounting procedures.*

2. This word group is a phrase because it lacks a subject, a complete verb, and a sense of completion. A revision could be the following: *Thank you for your letter of May 6 concerning our hiring policies.*

3. This example has a subject, *the report*. The rest of the word group is a dependent clause. The word group lacks a complete verb and a sense of completion. Revisions could be the following: *The report was completed by the April 15 deadline only through the hard work and long hours of the entire staff.*

   Or

   *I was proud of the report, which was completed by the April 15 deadline only through the hard work and long hours of the entire staff.*

4. The first word group is a fragment; it has a subject, *The approach*, and a dependent clause, but lacks a complete verb and a sense of completion. The second word group is a complete sentence. By deleting the word *that* in the first word group, you can make the sentence complete as follows: *The approach was recommended by the consultants whom we had contracted to solve the problem. In this approach, we increase the formal training of our analysts and hire an additional analyst.*

   Or you can combine the two word groups as follows:

   *In the approach that was recommended by the consultants whom we had contracted to solve the problem, we increase the formal training of our analysts and hire an additional analyst.*

5. The first word group is a fragment; it is a dependent clause. The second word group is a complete sentence. By deleting the word *after* at the beginning of the clause, you can make the dependent clause into an independent clause. *We studied the technical aspects of the proposal, and our contracts office reviewed its financial aspects. The proposal, although innovative, does not meet our immediate needs.*

# Confidence Check

Circle the letter of the word group that is a complete sentence. Identify the incomplete sentence in each pair as a clause or phrase.

1.

    a. If the results are not available by the close of business today.

    b. The results may not be available by the close of business today.

2.

    a. To travel by plane from Washington to Chicago and by train from Chicago to Cairo, which is at the southern tip of Illinois.

    b. It will be expensive to travel by plane from Washington to Chicago and by train from Chicago to Cairo.

3.

    a. Hearing the crackle and boom of lightning and thunder in the distance, I ran at once for the farmhouse.

    b. Hearing the crackle and boom of lightning and thunder in the distance.

4.

    a. Lucille Ball charmed American audiences for many years as a dizzy red-head with showbiz aspirations.

    b. Lucille Ball, who was beloved by American audiences for many years.

# Confidence Check Answers

1. b—Choice a is a dependent clause because it is introduced with the word *if*. Choice b is an independent clause.

2. b—Choice a begins with a phrase and ends with a dependent clause. Choice b is an independent clause.

3. a—Choice a begins with a phrase that is followed by an independent clause. Choice b is a phrase because it has no subject and an incomplete verb.

4. a—Choice a is an independent clause. Choice b begins with a subject for an independent clause, but is then followed by a dependent clause. The word group lacks a verb for the subject *Lucille Ball*.

# Confidence Check

Identify each of the following word groups as either a sentence fragment (F) or a complete sentence (C). If the word group is a fragment, make it a complete sentence.

1. While some people carefully consider the attributes of the candidates running for the presidency and often find the candidates lacking.

2. To install the new accounting software that we purchased because of its excellent rating by our information technology staff.

3. Considering that all of the books were ordered two months before the course's scheduled starting date.

4. A talented, well-educated spokesperson, who has a reputation of being fair and honest.

5. Pleased by the enthusiastic response to our course announcement, we decided to offer a second session.

# Possible Confidence Check Answers

1. F—This word group is a dependent clause. By dropping the word *while*, you can make the word group into an independent clause. *Some people carefully consider the attributes of the candidates running for the presidency and often find the candidates lacking.*

   Or you can add an independent clause after the dependent clause.

   *While some people carefully consider the attributes of the candidates running for the presidency and often find the candidates lacking, others vote a straight ticket without considering the candidates individually.*

2. F—This word group is a phrase because it lacks a subject, a complete verb, and a sense of completion. A possible revision would be to change the phrase to an independent clause by adding a subject, dropping the word *to*, and changing *install* to *installed*. *I installed the new accounting software that we purchased because of its excellent rating by our information technology staff.*

   Or you could add an independent clause after the introductory phrase.

   *To install the new accounting software that we purchased because of its excellent rating by our information technology staff, follow the step-by-step instructions in the manual.*

3. F—This word group is a phrase because it lacks a subject, a complete verb, and a sense of completion. By dropping *considering that*, you can make the phrase into an independent clause. *All of the books were ordered two months before the course's scheduled starting date.*

   Or you can add an independent clause after the introductory phrase.

   *Considering that all of the books were ordered two months before the course's scheduled starting date, they should have arrived by now.*

4. F—This word group is a phrase because it lacks a subject, a complete verb, and a sense of completion. By adding a subject and a verb, you can make the sentence have a sense of completion. *He is a talented, well-educated spokesperson, who has a reputation of being fair and honest.*

5. C—This word group is a phrase followed by an independent clause and is, therefore, correct.

# Run-on Sentences

A **run-on sentence** consists of two or more sentences (independent clauses) run together without a period or a semicolon or another terminal mark of punctuation to separate them.

Terminal marks of punctuation—!, ?, ., or ;—may be used to separate two independent clauses. (A comma by itself cannot be used between two independent clauses.)

Here are some examples of run-on sentences:

- ❒ The cruise ship is enormous, it weighs 142,000 tons and accommodates 3,114 passengers.

- ❒ The moon moved in front of the sun the eclipse began.

- ❒ Cara is shy she usually refuses all party invitations.

- ❒ Penguins are amusing and interesting birds, their natural habitat is the Antarctic.

- ❒ Reggie is a licensed attorney he has chosen to devote his life to his first love—teaching.

- ❒ We asked Professor Williams to look at the problem he is an expert in the field.

## Correcting the Run-on Sentence

To correct a run-on sentence, do one of the following:

1. Make the two independent clauses into separate sentences.

   - ❒ The cruise ship is enormous. It weighs 142,000 tons and accommodates 3,114 passengers.

2. Insert a comma and a coordinating conjunction after the first independent clause (IC). Be sure both word groups are complete sentences before putting a comma before the conjunction.

   | IC, for IC. | IC, but IC. | IC, yet IC. |
   |---|---|---|
   | IC, and IC. | IC, or IC. | IC, so IC. |
   | IC, nor IC. | | |

   - ❒ The moon moved in front of the sun, and the eclipse began.

3. Insert a semicolon between the two independent clauses.

   - ❒ Penguins are amusing and interesting birds; their natural habitat is the Antarctic.

4. Change one independent clause to a dependent clause.

   - ❒ Because Cara is shy, she usually refuses all party invitations.

5. Insert a semicolon after the first independent clause, a conjunctive adverb between the two independent clauses, and a comma after the conjunctive adverb.

   IC; however, IC.      IC; thus, IC.

   IC; moreover, IC.     IC; nevertheless, IC.

   IC; therefore, IC.    IC; consequently, IC.

   ❏ Reggie is a licensed attorney; however, he has chosen to devote his life to his first love—teaching.

6. Change one of the two independent clauses to a phrase.

   ❏ We asked Professor Williams, an expert in the field, to look at the problem.

# Confidence Check

Circle the letter of the item that contains a run-on sentence. (Two items in each set are punctuated correctly.) Identify the independent and dependent clauses in all items.

1.
   a. We enjoyed traveling Route 1 along the Pacific Ocean, the view of the mountains on the east and of the water on the west was breathtaking.
   b. We enjoyed traveling Route 1 along the Pacific Ocean where the mountains stretched along the east and the water stretched along the west.
   c. We enjoyed traveling Route 1 along the Pacific Ocean; the majestic mountains stretched along the east, and the water stretched along the west.

2.
   a. Time is all relative. Places that seem old to Americans often seem new to visitors from Europe.
   b. Time is all relative, places that seem old to Americans often seem new to Europeans.
   c. Because time is all relative, places that seem old to Americans often seem new to Europeans.

3.
   a. We were eager to get away from our everyday surroundings; our eyes hungered for new sights.
   b. We were eager to get away from our everyday surroundings and to see new sights.
   c. We were eager to get away from our everyday surroundings we longed to see new sights and meet new people.

4.
   a. Children can fill your life with joy and frustrations each one is a unique experience.
   b. Filling your life with joy and frustrations, each child is a unique experience.
   c. Each child is a unique experience, which can add both joy and frustrations to your life.

# Confidence Check Answers

1.  a—Choice a is a run-on sentence because a comma is not strong enough to separate two independent clauses. Choice b is correct because it is made up of one independent clause (*We enjoyed traveling Route 1 along the Pacific Ocean*) and one dependent clause (*where the mountains stretched along the east and the water stretched along the west*). Choice c is correct because the first two independent clauses are separated by a semicolon; the second two independent clauses are separated by the coordinating conjunction *and* and a comma.

2.  b—Choice b is a run-on sentence because a comma is not strong enough to separate two independent clauses. Choice a is correct because the two independent clauses are separated by a period. Choice a also has a dependent clause *(that seem old to Americans)* in the independent clause. Choice c is correct because it is made up of one dependent clause (*Because time is all relative*) and one independent clause (*places that seem old to Americans often seem new to Europeans*). The independent clause has a dependent clause *(that seem old to Americans)* within it.

3.  c—Choice c is a run-on sentence because there is no punctuation between the two independent clauses (*We were eager to get away from our everyday surroundings* and *we longed to see new sights and meet new people*). Choice a is correct because the two independent clauses are separated by a semicolon. Choice b is correct because it is one independent clause with two verbal (infinitive) phrases (to get away from our everyday surroundings and to see new sights and meet new people). The word group after the word *and* is not a complete sentence, so a comma should not precede *and*.

4.  a—Choice a is a run-on sentence because there is no punctuation between the two independent clauses (*Children can fill your life with joy and frustrations* and *each one is a unique experience*). Choice b is correct because the word group is one independent clause (*each child is a unique experience*) preceded by an introductory phrase (*Filling your life with joy and frustrations*). Choice c is correct because the sentence is made up of one independent clause (*Each child is a unique experience)* and one dependent clause (*which can add both joy and frustrations to your life*).

# Confidence Check

Decide if each item is a sentence fragment (F), a run-on sentence (R), or a complete sentence as written (C).

1. When we were young, naive, and full of untempered idealism about people and life.

2. As I raced toward the finish line, I turned to check the runner behind me and saw him pass me.

3. To realize our dreams and fulfill our potential at work and at home.

4. To own your own business, you must be motivated and organized.

5. Money does not guarantee happiness, happiness comes from the heart.

6. Books are our friends; they take us to foreign places, introduce us to interesting people, and provide many hours of fun and relaxation.

7. Having both parents of young children working outside the home presents a daily challenge because the children must be dressed, fed, and transported before the official work day begins.

8. Like many Americans, we own two foreign cars we have had too many problems with American-made cars.

9. The house contained four bedrooms, three bathrooms, a sun room, a library, a formal living room and dining room, and an eat-in kitchen.

10. Because our office equipment is outdated, the manager purchased twelve computers, two high-speed printers, a scanner, a color fax machine, and fourteen telephones.

# Confidence Check Answers

1. F—This word group is a dependent clause because it begins with the word *When*.

2. C—This word group is made up of one dependent clause (*As I raced toward the finish line*) and one independent clause (*I turned to check the runner behind me and saw him pass me*).

3. F—This word group is a phrase because it contains neither a subject nor a verb.

4. C—This word group is made up of an introductory phrase (*To own your own business*) and an independent clause (*you must be motivated and organized*).

5. R—This word group is made up of two independent clauses (*Money does not guarantee happiness* and *happiness comes from the heart*). A comma is not strong enough between two complete thoughts (independent clauses).

6. C—This word group is made up of two independent clauses (*Books are our friends* and *they take us to foreign places, introduce us to interesting people, and provide many hours of fun and relaxation*. A semicolon can separate two independent clauses.

7. C—This word group is made up of one independent clause (*Having both parents of young children working outside the home presents a daily challenge*) and two dependent clauses (*because the children must be dressed, fed, and transported* and *before the official work day begins*).

8. R—This word group is a run-on sentence because no punctuation separates the two independent clauses (*Like many Americans, we own two foreign cars* and *we have had too many problems with American-made cars*).

9. C—This word group is one independent clause.

10. C—This word group has one dependent clause (*Because our office equipment is outdated*) and one independent clause (*the manager purchased twelve computers, two high-speed printers, a scanner, a color fax machine, and fourteen telephones*).

# Confidence Check

Some of the following items contain sentence fragments. Edit each fragment by expanding it to a complete sentence or by connecting it to a complete sentence. If the passage contains only complete sentences, write *Correct*.

1. The scientist offered several examples to show how interesting chemistry can be. And to give me an idea of the kind of problems a chemist has to solve.

2. Finding a good job can be accomplished in a variety of ways. Through the Internet, the newspaper, friends and colleagues, a placement service, or cold calls.

3. At his first book signing appearance, the young novelist sold 200 copies of his book. Which was many more than he expected.

4. She has one purpose in life. Shopping for new shoes.

5. The flash flood warning that came on the television screen during the Nationals–Mets game. It caused quite a stir in the family.

6. Because the city policy on housing is confusing. Which is why we believe the proposed amendments should be passed.

7. If you want to be healthy. You should do two things: eat the right foods and exercise regularly.

8. Suzanna is energetic and creative. For example, her ideas for the upcoming conference being incorporated into Friday's program.

9. Mike exhibits the qualities of a good father. For example, he takes his children to ball games or on trips and listens attentively when his children speak to him.

10. They are moving into a condominium in a quiet neighborhood. Wanting a safe, peaceful environment.

# Possible Confidence Check Answers

1. The first word group is a complete sentence; the second is a fragment because it has no subject. One way to correct this sentence would be to combine the complete sentence with the fragment. *The scientist offered several examples to show how interesting chemistry can be and to give me an idea of the kind of problems a chemist has to solve.*

2. The first word group is a complete sentence; the second is a fragment because it is a prepositional phrase. This list could follow a colon at the end of the independent clause. *Finding a good job can be accomplished in a variety of ways: through the Internet, the newspaper, friends and colleagues, a placement service, or cold calls.*

3. The first word group is a complete sentence; the second is a fragment because it is a dependent clause. The error can be corrected by combing the two word groups. *At his first book signing appearance, the young novelist sold 200 copies of his book, which was many more than he expected.*

4. The first word group is a complete sentence; the second is a fragment because it is a phrase. The phrase can be added to the independent clause. *She has one purpose in life: shopping for new shoes.*

5. The first word group is a fragment because it has a main subject but no verb and a dependent clause; the second word group is a complete sentence. The two word groups can be combined as follows: *The flash flood warning that came on the television screen during the Nationals–Mets game caused quite a stir in the family.*

6. Both word groups are fragments. Each is a dependent clause. The fragment can be corrected by keeping the first dependent clause and changing the second on to an independent clause: *Because the city policy on housing is confusing, the city council members are hoping the proposed amendment will pass.*

7. The first word group is a fragment because it is a dependent clause; the second is a complete sentence. The error can be corrected by combining the two word groups. *If you want to be healthy, you should do two things: eat the right foods and exercise regularly.*

8. The first word group is a complete sentence; the second is a fragment because it has a subject but no verb and a dependent clause. The error can be corrected by adding *are* before *being*. *Suzanna is energetic and creative. For example, her ideas for the upcoming conference are being incorporated into Friday's program.*

9. This passage is correct because it has two independent clauses.

10. The first word group is a complete sentence; the second is a fragment because it is a phrase. The error can be corrected by changing the phrase to a dependent clause and attaching it to the first sentence. *They are moving into a condominium in a quiet neighborhood because they want a safe, peaceful environment.*

# Confidence Check

Some of the following items contain run-on sentences. Correct the run-on sentences by rewriting the passage or by using the appropriate punctuation between complete sentences. If the sentence is correct, write *Correct*.

1. Evidence continues to mount it shows that passive smoke causes diseases.

2. Dr. Ling is the director of the hospital he also maintains a private practice.

3. We exited the ramp in the wrong direction, we drove 20 miles before we realized our error.

4. She is very committed to her work, she rarely leaves work at the scheduled ending time.

5. Stevie Wonder was "discovered" at the age of 11, he signed on with Motown under the stage name of Little Stevie Wonder.

6. The airline gave a discount on the Atlanta flight, but the number of passengers continued to decline.

7. Whether it is regulating national banks, determining international economic policy, collecting income and excise taxes, issuing securities, reporting the government's daily financial transactions, or manufacturing coins or bills for circulation, the one concern that still ties together the activities of the Department of the Treasury is money.

# Possible Confidence Check Answers

1.  This word group is a run-on sentence because there is no punctuation separating the two independent clauses. One way to correct the error would be to make one of the independent clauses into a phrase. *Evidence continues to mount showing that passive smoke causes diseases.*

    Or you could use a semicolon (or a period) to separate the two independent clauses. *Evidence continues to mount; it shows that passive smoke causes diseases.*

2.  This word group is a run-on sentence because there is no punctuation separating the two independent clauses. You could use a semicolon (or a period) to separate the two independent clauses. *Dr. Ling is the director of the hospital; he also maintains a private practice.*

    Or you could make one of the independent clauses into a dependent clause. *Although Dr. Ling is the director of the hospital, he also maintains a private practice.*

3.  This word group is a run-on sentence because there is no punctuation separating the two independent clauses. You could use a semicolon (or a period) to separate the two independent clauses. *We exited the ramp in the wrong direction; we drove 20 miles before we realized our error.*

    Or you could combine the sentences into one independent clause with a compound verb by deleting the second *we*. *We exited the ramp in the wrong direction and drove 20 miles before we realized our error.*

4.  This word group is a run-on sentence because a comma is not strong enough to separate two independent clauses. You could use a semicolon and a conjunctive adverb to join the two independent clauses. *She is very committed to her work; therefore, she rarely leaves work at the scheduled ending time.*

    Or you could change the first independent clause into a dependent clause. *Because she is very committed to her work, she rarely leaves work at the scheduled ending time.*

5.  This word group is a run-on sentence because a comma is not strong enough to separate two independent clauses. You could make the information in the first independent clause into a modifying phrase. *Stevie Wonder, "discovered" at the age of 11, signed a contract with Motown under the stage name of Little Stevie Wonder.*

6.  This sentence is correct because two independent clauses are joined by a comma and the coordinating conjunction *but*.

7.  This sentence is correct because the first part is a dependent clause *(Whether it is regulating national banks, determining international economic policy, collecting income and excise taxes, issuing securities, reporting the government's daily financial transactions, or manufacturing coins or bills for circulation),* and the second part is an independent clause *(the one concern that still ties together the activities of the Department of the Treasury is money).*

# Module 3: Punctuation

Does this word group make any sense to you?

☐ That that is is that that is not is not is that it it is.

I hope not. Now, notice what happens when I insert punctuation.

☐ That that is, is. That that is not, is not. Is that it? It is.

Now that I have used punctuation and some capitalization, the passage makes sense. Punctuation marks are symbols that help readers understand the material they are reading. Punctuation offers the reader various signals: stop, pause, this information is important, this information can be skipped, this noun owns that noun, etc.

Used correctly, punctuation is a guiding light; used incorrectly, punctuation is a shot in the dark.

# Commas

The comma is probably the most used, overused, and misused form of punctuation. For some reason, writers often suffer from comma angst. I have no magic formula for learning comma rules; they are many. Some may even be a judgment call. But even so, you must be able to go to a rule to support any change you make. Once you understand a rule for the comma—again that's understand, not memorize—you will be able to make a generalization about the rule and apply it to your writing, editing, or proofreading.

## Commas with Independent and Dependent Clauses

Two independent clauses can be connected with a comma and a coordinating conjunction (*and, but, for, or, nor, yet,* and sometimes *so.*)

❏ She was a welcome guest in our home, and she always made us feel we were the perfect hosts.

Use a comma to set off an introductory dependent clause. A dependent clause contains both a subject and a verb, but it is incapable of standing alone as a sentence because of the word introducing the clause. Words that commonly introduce dependent clauses include *when, that, as, if, unless, although, after, because, since, until, though.*

❏ Because we cut the budget, we will not be able to hire any new staff members this year.

Do not use a comma to set off most adverbial dependent clauses at the end of a sentence unless the clause is parenthetical. Adverbial clauses answer one of the following questions: *How? Why? Where? To what degree? What direction? In what manner?*

❏ We will not be able to hire any new staff members this year because we cut the budget.

# Confidence Check

Study the punctuation of the dependent and independent clauses in the following sentences. If the punctuation is correct, write "Correct" next to the sentence. If the punctuation is incorrect, correct it. You may add conjunctions as necessary.

1. I was offered a salary higher than my current one but the hours were much longer.

2. The manuscript needed a full-time editor and a full-time proofreader, the project manager realized the project would take longer than first anticipated.

3. I laughed at his suggestions; however, I later realized his ideas were not so ridiculous and could be incorporated into our plan.

4. My brother loves to cook but he hates to clean up the kitchen.

5. The report was missing some important information because we misunderstood the directions.

6. The truck driver signaled cautiously, and turned left.

7. We cannot guarantee you a place in this class, unless you enroll today.

8. While we were eating the dog spilled all of her water.

9. We would like to be available when the injured arrive.

10. The candidates will be given a written exam; and those who qualify will be offered an internship.

# Confidence Check Answers

1. I was offered a salary higher than my current one, but the hours were much longer. (Because this sentence is composed of two independent clauses, a comma is placed before the coordinating conjunction.)

2. The manuscript needed a full-time editor and a full-time proofreader; the project manager realized the project would take longer than first anticipated. (A semicolon or a period could be placed between the two independent clauses.)

3. I laughed at his suggestions; however, I later realized his ideas were not so ridiculous and could be incorporated into our plan. (These two independent clauses are correctly joined with a semicolon, a conjunctive adverb, and a comma.)

4. My brother loves to cook, but he hates to clean up the kitchen. (A comma is needed before the coordinating conjunction that joins the two independent clauses.)

5. The report was missing some important information because we misunderstood the directions. (This sentence is correct because the dependent clause, *because we misunderstood the directions*, is at the end of the sentence.)

6. The truck driver signaled cautiously and turned left. (This sentence should have no comma because the conjunction *and* joins two verbs, not two independent clauses.)

7. We cannot guarantee you a place in this class unless you enroll today. (This sentence should have no comma because the dependent clause, *unless you enroll today*, is at the end of the sentence.)

8. While we were eating, the dog spilled all of her water. (A comma should be placed after an introductory dependent clause. In addition, without the comma, someone could on first reading think that someone was eating the dog. Remember, if someone has to read the sentence more than once to understand it, then there is something wrong with the sentence.)

9. We would like to be available when the injured arrive. (This sentence is correct because the dependent clause, *when the injured arrive* is at the end of the sentence.)

10. The candidates will be given a written exam, and those who qualify will be offered an internship. (Because this sentence is composed of two independent clauses, the semicolon should be replaced with a comma before the coordinating conjunction.)

# Confidence Check

Correct any errors in the punctuation of independent and dependent clauses. Use sentence patterns to help you make your corrections.

Being a working mother is not easy, she is expected to wear two

hats at the same time. One hat is that of "Mother." Mother is

always there to nurture her children and she puts the needs of her children above all

else. She is aware of the outside world; but home and family take priority in her life.

The second hat is that of "Professional Woman." The professional woman excels on

the job, and is expected to stay late to finish projects. Because these two sets of

responsibilities have conflicting expectations the working mother must often make

choices that affect her success in her two jobs.

# Possible Confidence Check Answers

Being a working mother is not easy; she is expected to wear two hats at the same time. One hat is that of "Mother." Mother is always there to nurture her children, and she puts the needs of her children above all else. She is aware of the outside world, but home and family take priority in her life. The second hat is that of "Professional Woman." The professional woman excels on the job and is expected to stay late to finish projects. Because these two sets of responsibilities have conflicting expectations, the working mother must often make choices that affect her success in her two jobs.

Line 1—a semicolon (or a period) is needed after the word *easy* to separate the two independent clauses.

Line 3—a comma is needed before the coordinate conjunction *and* to join two independent clauses.

Line 4—the semicolon after *world* should be a comma (or the word *but* should be deleted and the semicolon retained) because the comma and the conjunction *but* join the two independent clauses.

Line 6—The comma after *job* should be deleted because the word *and* is joining two verbs, not two independent clauses.

Line 7—A comma is inserted after *expectations* because the sentence begins with a dependent clause.

# Commas after Introductory Constructions

Commas are used to set off most types of introductory constructions. Introductory constructions are words, phrases, or clauses used at the beginning of a sentence or at the beginning of an independent clause elsewhere in the sentence.

**Set off an introductory dependent clause with a comma.** We have already discussed setting off a dependent clause when it appears at the beginning of a sentence. A dependent clause introduced by a subordinating conjunction is usually not set off when it appears at the end of a sentence.

❏ Although punctuation may seem arbitrary, most rules are closely related to meaning.

Note that *although* makes the first clause dependent. The comma after *arbitrary* helps make the independent clause stand out.

Remember to place a comma after a dependent clause that introduces an independent clause in the middle of a sentence.

❏ I walked to the library to get Anita Shreve's new book, but when I arrived, all copies had already been checked out.

Note that the preceding sentence begins with an independent clause. *But* joins the first independent clause with a second independent clause, which itself is made up of one dependent clause and one independent clause. A comma is placed after *book* because it introduces an independent clause and makes the independent clause stand out. Remember, more important information should be in the independent clause.

**Use a comma to set off an introductory verbal phrase.** A verbal phrase is a word group containing a verb form that is used as another part of speech and has no subject. The infinitive is the *to* form of the verb (*to walk, to begin*). An infinitive can function as an adjective, adverb, or noun. Verbs have two participle forms: the present and the past. The present participle ends in *–ing* (*walking, beginning*); the past participle ends with *–ed* or an irregular form (*walked, begun*). Both the present and past participles function as adjectives. A comma follows introductory verbal phrases that function as adjectives or adverbs.

Here are examples of verbal phrases.

❏ **Infinitive phrase:** To learn to play the guitar properly, you must take lessons and practice every day.

❏ **Present participial phrase:** Offering tender loving care, the nurse was a favorite among the patients on the pediatric ward.

❏ **Past participial phrase:** Embarrassed by his ill-spoken words, he quickly changed the subject.

**Use a comma to set off transitional words and phrases.** Transitions are words or phrases at the beginning of a sentence that help connect the sentence to the preceding sentence.

Here are examples of transitional words and phrases.

❑ Finally, the seniors will participate in an all-night grad party.

❑ In the meantime, you may use the computer in the lab.

❑ As a result, we can all enjoy an extra day off.

**Most grammar references discourage writers from setting off short introductory words or phrases that refer to time or place.** *Short* usually means one to three words. Some references say one to four words. Some organizations' style manuals direct writers, editors, and proofreaders to place a comma after these short phrases. Be sure to be consistent.

Here are examples of short phrases of time and place that should not be followed by a comma.

❑ In 2017 we received a supplemental appropriation to enforce the new regulation.

❑ On Tuesday we will meet to discuss the proposed downsizing.

❑ In my office I have the client's most recent draft of the proposal.

❑ Today we received the material that should have been delivered yesterday.

The exceptions to this rule include sentences that could be misread without the comma and sentences beginning with three-part dates. Note that the year in a three-part date should always be set off with commas, no matter where it is in a sentence. When two numbers are next to each other, they should be separated by a comma.

Here are examples of short phrases of time and place that should be followed by a comma.

❑ In 2017, 300 people attended the retirement workshops.

❑ On October 28, 2017, the committee met to discuss the risks of drug XYZ.

# Confidence Check

For each sentence, decide whether the italicized introductory construction should be followed by a comma.

1. *Dancing gracefully across the floor* she charmed the spectators.

2. *On July 1* my lease expires.

3. *In my office* I have a computer and a laser printer.

4. *In other words* my supervisor wants to fire me.

5. *Because the contractor made a mistake* I won the court case.

6. *Threatened by the stick* the stray dog ran away.

7. *Unless she successfully completes the required course* she will not graduate in June.

8. *Nevertheless* I am determined to travel to Alaska this winter.

9. *To find my office* go to the end of the main corridor and turn left.

10. *For my last point* I will describe the importance of aerobic exercise.

11. *Declining her party's nomination for governor,* the state senator was clear that she wanted to complete her present term.

12. *Requisitioned by my predecessor* the chair is too large for me.

13. *Above all* we must meet the deadlines.

# Confidence Check Answers

1. *Dancing gracefully across the floor,* she charmed the spectators. (A comma is placed after an introductory present participial phrase.)

2. *On July 1* my lease expires. (No comma is placed after a short phrase of time.)

3. *In my office* I have a computer and a laser printer. (No comma is placed after a short phrase of place.)

4. *In other words,* my supervisor wants to fire me. (A comma is placed after an introductory transitional phrase.)

5. *Because the contractor made a mistake,* I won the court case. (A comma is placed after an introductory dependent clause.)

6. *Threatened by the stick,* the stray dog ran away. (A comma is placed after an introductory past participial phrase.)

7. *Unless she successfully completes the required course,* she will not graduate in June. (A comma is placed after an introductory dependent clause.)

8. *Nevertheless,* I am determined to travel to Alaska this winter. (A comma is placed after an introductory transitional word.)

9. *To find my office,* go to the end of the main corridor and turn left. (A comma is placed after an introductory infinitive phrase.)

10. *For my last point,* I will describe the importance of aerobic exercise. (A comma is placed after an introductory transitional phrase.)

11. *Declining her party's nomination for governor,* the state senator was clear that she wanted to complete her present term. (A comma is placed after an introductory present participial phrase.)

12. *Requisitioned by my predecessor,* the chair is too large for me. (A comma is placed after an introductory past participial phrase.)

13. *Above all,* we must meet the deadlines. (A comma is placed after an introductory transitional phrase.)

# Confidence Check

Write "Correct" if a sentence is punctuated correctly. Write "Incorrect" if a sentence is punctuated incorrectly. Then correct the punctuation problem, and state a reason for your correction.

1. As mentioned on page 7, we must adopt the new procedure for four reasons.

2. Finally purchasing a new computer system will be cost-effective.

3. Created by the team of experts from IBM the new software addresses all our computer needs.

4. On the other hand no new procedure will have all smooth sailing.

5. Having visited New York once this year I had no desire to go there again.

6. While reaching for the milk pitcher, I knocked over my glass.

7. Because she has 15 years' experience in the marketing field I recommend that we offer her the marketing director position.

8. In addition she has had extensive Internet experience.

9. To feel confident about opening day you should practice your lines every night.

10. In fact performing for your family can be fun.

11. Looking up in the sky, I was able to see the eclipse of the moon.

12. If you are unable to make the rehearsal on Friday, please talk to the stage manager.

13. Last year I was promoted to senior editor.

14. On April 1, 2016, I came to work for this organization.

15. In my office I have the books you will need for your project.

16. On March 22 25 people from our company will attend the seminar at the Hilton.

17. Moreover we have had the support of our supervisors in all of our efforts.

18. After the argument was over we laughed at ourselves for being so upset about nothing.

19. To participate in the soccer tournament he had to wear a knee brace.

20. With only 130 passengers aboard the plane was half full.

21. Expecting a green and tree-filled campus I was surprised to find a university surrounded by highways and parking lots.

22. Because rural areas have an insufficient number of dentists, many residents cannot get treatment.

23. While reviewing the text Hillary noticed dozens of typographical errors.

# Confidence Check Answers

1. Correct. A comma must follow an introductory transitional phrase.

2. Incorrect. A comma must follow an introductory transitional word. *Finally, ....*

3. Incorrect. A comma must follow a past participial phrase. *Created by the team of experts from IBM, ....*

4. Incorrect. A comma must follow an introductory transitional phrase. *On the other hand, ....*

5. Incorrect. A comma must follow an introductory present participial phrase. *Having visited New York once this year, ....*

6. Correct. A comma must follow an introductory phrase.

7. Incorrect. A comma must follow an introductory dependent clause. *Because she has 15 years' experience in the marketing field, ....*

8. Incorrect. A comma must follow an introductory transitional phrase. *In addition, ....*

9. Incorrect. A comma must follow an introductory infinitive phrase. *To feel confident about opening day, ....*

10. Incorrect. A comma must follow an introductory transitional phrase. *In fact, ....*

11. Correct. A comma must follow an introductory participial phrase.

12. Correct. A comma must follow an introductory dependent clause.

13. Correct. A comma does not follow a short introductory phrase of time.

14. Correct. A comma follows an introductory three-part date.

15. Correct. A comma does not follow a short introductory phrase of place.

16. Incorrect. A comma must follow a short introductory phrase of time if the sentence could be misread. *On March 22, ....*

17. Incorrect. A comma must follow an introductory transitional word. *Moreover, ....*

18. Incorrect. A comma must follow an introductory dependent clause. *After the argument was over, ....*

19. Incorrect. A comma must follow an introductory infinitive phrase. *To participate in the soccer tournament, ....*

20. Incorrect. A comma must follow an introductory phrase if the sentence could be misread on first reading. *With only 130 passengers aboard, ....*

21. Incorrect. A comma must follow an introductory present participial phrase. *Expecting a green and tree-filled campus, ....*

22. Correct. A comma must follow an introductory dependent clause.

23. Incorrect. A comma must follow an introductory phrase. *While reviewing the text, ....*

# Confidence Check

Using the guidelines in this section, add or delete commas after introductory constructions. State a reason for your changes.

1. First of all let me be honest. I am no expert in writing, but I do know one thing. The purpose of writing is to communicate a message. However writers often fail to communicate effectively with their readers.

2. Because I proofread many letters I often see examples of failed communication. On January 18 I proofread a long letter to a senator. While proofreading the first page I found five grammar errors. Moreover I found two punctuation errors on the second page. On the last page, there were three spelling errors. If I had not caught these errors they would have annoyed the senator and created a negative image of our agency.

3. On my desk, I have a stack of letters to proofread. Written in answer to a consumer complaint one letter begins as follows: "The claims you made in your letter of December 21 were outrageous." If that letter is mailed the recipient will probably not read beyond the first paragraph.

4. Just written yesterday another letter refers to an incoming letter written three months ago as "your recent letter." In the six pages that follow the writer fails to state the purpose of the letter. In my view the letter is not worth sending as written.

# Confidence Check Answers

1. First of all, *(a comma should follow an introductory transitional phrase)* let me be honest. I am no expert in writing, but I do know one thing. The purpose of writing is to communicate a message. However, *(a comma should follow an introductory transitional word)* writers often fail to communicate effectively with their readers.

2. Because I proofread many letters, *(a comma should follow an introductory dependent clause)* I often see examples of failed communication. On January 18 I proofread a long letter to a senator. While proofreading the first page, *(a comma should follow an introductory phrase)* I found five grammar errors. Moreover, *(a comma should follow an introductory transitional word)* I found two punctuation errors on the second page. On the last page, there were three spelling errors. If I had not caught these errors, *(a comma should follow an introductory dependent clause)* they would have annoyed the senator and created a negative image of our agency.

3. On my desk *(no comma should follow a short phrase of place)* I have a stack of letters to proofread. Written in answer to a consumer complaint, *(a comma should follow an introductory past participial phrase)* one letter begins as follows: "The claims you made in your letter of December 21 were outrageous." If that letter is mailed, *(a comma should follow an introductory dependent clause)* the recipient will probably not read beyond the first paragraph.

4. Just written yesterday, *(a comma should follow an introductory past participial phrase)* another letter refers to an incoming letter written three months ago as "your recent letter." In the six pages that follow, *(a comma should follow an introductory transitional phrase)* the writer fails to state the purpose of the letter. In my view, *(a comma should follow an introductory transitional phrase)* the letter is not worth sending as written.

# Commas with Nonrestrictive Material

Commas should be used to isolate words that are not necessary to the meaning of the sentence. Think of commas as handles. They can be used to lift nonessential information from a sentence. Nonessential words, phrases, and clauses can be lifted out of a sentence, and the meaning of the sentence will not be affected. Another term for nonessential is *nonrestrictive*. Without the nonrestrictive information between the commas, the sentence will still make sense.

Nonrestrictive expressions are set off with two commas: one before the expression and one after it. If the expression ends the sentence, use only the comma before the expression.

       ❏ My goal, of course, is to keep my children on the four-year college plan.

In the sentence above, the phrase *of course* is not essential to the meaning of the sentence. Thus, it is separated from the rest of the sentence by two commas. The commas show the reader that the phrase is nonessential.

There are five types of nonrestrictive word groups: **interrupters**, **parenthetical phrases or clauses**, **explanatory elements**, **appositives**, and *such as* **constructions**.

## Interrupters

Interrupters are words or phrases that interrupt a sentence. You can hear interrupters when you read aloud because your volume and pitch drop. You may also hear a pause. On paper, you must have an indicator that a pause or a break is needed, thus, the commas. Interrupters are nonrestrictive.

The following are examples of words and phrases that can interrupt a sentence:

| | |
|---|---|
| as always | nevertheless |
| consequently | of course |
| for example | on the other hand |
| however | therefore |
| moreover | |

Below are some examples of nonrestrictive interrupters. For practice, you can read these sentences aloud and listen to the changes in your voice.

       ❏ Nothing annoys me more, however, than someone not telling the truth.

       ❏ My uncle, on the other hand, reads about all the candidates before he commits his support.

       ❏ Her first draft, for example, shows logical thinking.

You may have noticed that the words listed as interrupters can also appear as introductory constructions. You may have also noticed that words such as *however, therefore, moreover,* and *nevertheless* are punctuated differently when they interrupt an independent clause. These words have two different functions in the language. They can function as conjunctive adverbs that join two independent clauses, or they can function as interrupters in one independent clause. The following sentences illustrate two different uses of the same word.

**Interrupter:** Samuel Clemens, *however*, signed up as an apprentice to a steamboat pilot.

**Conjunctive adverb:** Orion Clemens became a printer; *however*, his brother Samuel signed on as an apprentice to a steamboat pilot.

# Parenthetical Phrases or Clauses

Parenthetical phrases or clauses are inserted in the sentence as additional comments. Although these comments may add emphasis, point out contrasts, or slightly modify the original statement, the meaning of the sentence is complete without them. Parenthetical expressions are nonrestrictive.

Here are some examples of nonrestrictive parenthetical phrases or clauses.

- ❏ The snare drum, not the kettle drum, carries the main beat in most modern music.

- ❏ The oboist, everyone was willing to concede, stole the show.

# Explanatory Elements

Explanatory elements, both clauses and phrases, modify a noun. Sometimes they are nonrestrictive. To determine if the explanatory element is nonrestrictive, read the sentence without the phrase or clause in question. If the meaning of the sentence has not changed, then the explanatory element is nonrestrictive. Use one comma before the explanatory information and one comma after the information. If the meaning of the sentence has changed, then the explanatory element is restrictive. In other words, it restricts or limits the meaning of the noun it modifies. Do not use commas.

Pay particular attention to dependent clauses beginning with *who, whom, which, that,* and *where.* If you are editing a piece and you are not sure from the context whether the information is restrictive or nonrestrictive, you will have to query the author.

Below are some examples of nonrestrictive explanatory elements.

- ❏ Our new administrative assistant, who used to be an English teacher, corrects me when I make grammar errors. (We have only one new administrative assistant.)

- ❏ My sister, who lives in New York, writes for public television. (I have only one sister.)

- ❏ Our old house, which we purchased in 1969, has been razed to make room for a new road. (We have only one old house.)

- ❏ The final proposal, edited by Meryl, was submitted to George for his approval. (There is only one final proposal.)

Here are some examples of restrictive explanatory elements.

- ❏ Our company seldom hires people who do not know at least three programming languages. (If we placed a comma before *who*, the sentence would mean our company seldom hires any people. The who clause is necessary to restrict the discussion to only the people who do not know three programming languages.)

❐ The manual *containing our company's style rules* is on my bookshelf. (The phrase *containing our company's style rules* explains exactly which manual the writer is talking about.)

❐ The car *that we purchased last month* has already been towed twice. (The clause *that we purchased last month* explains exactly which car the writer is talking about. The writer owns at least two cars.)

Note how the meaning of a sentence can change when commas are removed or inserted around an explanatory element. Both of the following sentences are correct, but they communicate two different messages.

❐ We are opposed to a cut in taxes, which could harm our public schools. (We are opposed to any cut in taxes.)

❐ We are opposed to a cut in taxes that could harm our public schools. (We are opposed to only one type of tax cut.)

The American convention is to use *which* for nonrestrictive clauses and *that* for restrictive clauses. (This is not true in British English where *which* is used in both restrictive and nonrestrictive clauses.) Use a comma before and after *which* clauses; do not use a comma before and after *that* clauses.

# Appositives

An appositive is a noun or noun phrase that identifies or gives additional information about a preceding noun or pronoun. An appositive can be nonrestrictive (use commas) or restrictive (do not use commas). To determine if commas are needed, read the sentence without the appositive. If the appositive can be omitted without changing the meaning of the sentence, use commas. If the appositive cannot be omitted, do not use commas.

Here are some examples of nonrestrictive appositives.

❐ Mindy Wagman, our computer guru, will explain our new operating system. (The phrase *our computer guru* is nonessential information because it does not affect the meaning of the sentence. Therefore, it is set off with commas.)

❐ Their new home, a ten-acre estate in Pine Plains, used to belong to a prominent South American developer. (The phrase *a ten-acre estate in Pine Plains* is nonessential information as it does not affect the meaning of the sentence. Therefore, it is set off with commas.)

Here are some examples of restrictive appositives.

❐ The poet Robert Frost writes about taking the less traveled road. (The name *Robert Frost* is essential to the meaning of the sentence. Without the poet's name, the reader would not know what poet is being discussed. The name is essential to the meaning of the sentence.)

❐ The book *The Shining* was made into a scary movie. (The name *The Shining* is essential to the meaning of the sentence. Without the book's name, the reader would not know what book is being discussed. The title is essential to the meaning of the sentence.)

## *Such as* Constructions

Place a comma before a phrase beginning with *such as* if the phrase is nonrestrictive, which is usually the case. Do not put any punctuation after *such as.*

Here are examples of nonrestrictive *such as* constructions.

Be alert for common errors, such as transposed words, repeating words, and missing words.

He recommended taking an appropriate communications course, such as "Effective Speaking," "Overcoming Communication Barriers," or "Persuasive Writing."

Note that in both sentences, the *such as* phrases are nonessential to the meaning of the sentence.

## Confidence Check

Identify the italicized element in each sentence as restrictive (R) or nonrestrictive (N) and change the punctuation as needed. Remember, set off nonrestrictive elements with commas. Do not set off restrictive elements.

1. Stores in states *where temperatures are mild* have no demand for heavy fur coats.

2. Our company will *of course* supply all of the materials needed for the project.

3. The time has come, *the committee agreed*, to rewrite the sick leave policy.

4. Ergonomically correct work stations are desirable for, *but not absolutely necessary to*, the comfort of the computer user.

5. He stated *moreover* that negative politics would have no place in his campaign.

6. Our new apartment building, *which we moved to last month*, does not yet have the parking lot paved.

7. Only the art pieces, *showing superior workmanship*, should be entered in the competition.

8. My oldest brother, *who just moved to Europe*, is studying at the Sorbonne.

9. My best friend, *a professor at the local university,* used to work in corporate America.

10. The composer *Stravinsky* created music *that was viewed as revolutionary in his time*.

# Confidence Check Answers

1. R—Stores in states *where temperatures are mild* have no demand for heavy fur coats. (Without the clause *where temperatures are mild* the sentence would make no sense. Try reading it without the clause.)

2. N—Our company will, *of course,* supply all of the materials needed for the project. (The phrase is nonessential because it does not affect the meaning of the sentence.)

3. N—The time has come, *the committee agreed*, to rewrite the sick leave policy. (The phrase is nonessential because it does not affect the meaning of the sentence.)

4. N—Ergonomically correct work stations are desirable for, *but not absolutely necessary to*, the comfort of the computer user. (The phrase is nonessential because it does not affect the meaning of the sentence.)

5. N—He stated, *moreover,* that the negative politics would have no place in his campaign. (The word is nonessential because it does not affect the meaning of the sentence.)

6. N—Our new apartment building, *which we moved to last month*, does not yet have the parking lot paved. (The clause is nonessential because it does not affect the meaning of the sentence.)

7. R—Only the art pieces *showing superior workmanship* should be entered in the competition. (The phrase is essential because it affects the meaning of the sentence. Try reading the sentence without the phrase. By using the restrictive phrase, the writer indicates exactly which art pieces should be entered into the competition.)

8. N—My oldest brother, *who just moved to Europe*, is studying at the Sorbonne. (The clause is nonessential because it does not affect the meaning of the sentence. The writer has already identified which brother is being discussed by using the word *oldest*.)

9. N—My best friend, *a professor at the local university,* used to work in corporate America. (The phrase is nonessential because it does not affect the meaning of the sentence. The profession of the friend is nonessential information.)

10. R—The composer *Stravinsky* created music *that was viewed as revolutionary in his time*. (The name *Stravinsky* is essential for the meaning of the sentence. Otherwise, the reader would not know what composer the writer is discussing. The clause is also restrictive because it tells the reader what kind of music is being discussed.)

# Confidence Check

In the following sentences, add or delete commas as necessary. Some sentences may require more than one comma. Explain your reason for your change. Also check for the correct use of *which* and *that*. If the sentence is already punctuated correctly, write "Correct."

1. The Hudson River which flows west of Manhattan is muddy and full of trash.

2. My new car which I purchased last month has already been towed twice.

3. In five minutes she solved the problem, that I had been working on for three hours.

4. A parking ticket is a summons, that is affixed by a police officer to a car or another vehicle and requires the motorist's response.

5. In the new Picasso Museum in Paris, the tourist can see many of Picasso's paintings that were given to the French government to pay back taxes.

6. President Kennedy's inaugural address that stirred the nation has now become a classic in rhetoric classes.

7. The house, which I lived in as a child, is about to be torn down as part of urban revitalization in Baltimore.

8. Please return all the textbooks, which I loaned to you last week.

9. My business office which is located in my home has become cluttered with boxes and boxes of books and papers.

10. My uncle, who lives in Mississippi, will visit us during the holidays.

11. The orchestra, playing patriotic music, captivated the audience.

12. This novel, which is my favorite, has been on the best-seller list for months.

13. In 2001 the American Youth Philharmonic was led by Leonard Slatkin, conductor of the National Symphony Orchestra in the Concert Hall at the Kennedy Center.

14. They are after all expecting a good show for their money.

15. A new hit television series on ABC on Sunday nights a fast-paced drama has helped lift the ratings of the network.

# Confidence Check Answers

1. The Hudson River, which flows west of Manhattan, is muddy and full of trash. (Read the sentence without the *which* clause and the meaning stays the same.)

2. My new car, which I purchased last month, has already been towed twice. (Assuming I have only one new car, the meaning of the sentence does not change when the which clause is deleted.)

3. The clause in this sentence could be either restrictive or nonrestrictive.

   In five minutes she solved the problem that I had been working on for three hours. (Deleting the comma and making the clause restrictive indicates that she was working on at least two problems. The sentence is discussing only the one that she had been working on for three hours. A comma should not precede a restrictive clause beginning with *that*.)

   In five minutes she solved the problem, which I had been working on for 3 hours. (Changing *that* to *which* indicates that this problem was the only one that she was working on. The nonrestrictive clause states extra information, the length of time that she had been working on the problem. A comma should precede a nonrestrictive clause beginning with *which*.)

4. A parking ticket is a summons that is affixed by a police officer to a car or another vehicle and requires the motorist's response. (Without the *that* clause, this sentence is unclear. There are all types of summons. A parking ticket is a specific type. A comma should not precede a restrictive clause beginning with *that*.)

5. In the new Picasso Museum in Paris, the tourist can see many of Picasso's paintings that were given to the French government to pay back taxes. (This sentence is correct. The restrictive *that* clause is needed to indicate which paintings tourists can see.)

6. President Kennedy's inaugural address, which stirred the nation, has now become a classic in rhetoric classes. (Because President Kennedy gave only one inaugural address, the clause is nonrestrictive. Therefore, the clause should begin with *which* and be set off with commas.)

7. The house that I lived in as a child is about to be torn down as part of urban revitalization in Baltimore. (Try reading the sentence without the clause. The reader would not know what house is being torn down. Therefore, the clause is essential to the meaning of the sentence. The clause should begin with *that* and should not be set off with commas.)

8. The clause in this sentence could be either restrictive or nonrestrictive.

   Please return all the textbooks that I loaned to you last week. (This is a restrictive clause because the writer wants only the textbooks that were loaned last week, no others.)

   Please return all the textbooks, which I loaned to you last week. (This is a nonrestrictive clause because the writer wants all the textbooks returned. They were all loaned last week.)

9. The clause in this sentence could be either restrictive or nonrestrictive.

   My business office, which is located in my home, has become cluttered with boxes and boxes of books and papers. (If I have only one business office, the use of *which* is correct. The clause should be set off with commas because it is nonrestrictive.)

My business office that is located in my home has become cluttered with boxes and boxes of books and papers. (If I have two businesses office, one in my home and one elsewhere, the use of *that* is correct. The clause should not be set off with commas because it is restrictive.)

10. The clause in this sentence could be either restrictive or nonrestrictive.

    My uncle, who lives in Mississippi, will visit us during the holidays. (If I have only one uncle, this sentence is correct.)

    My uncle who lives in Mississippi will visit us during the holidays. (If I have at least two uncles, the commas should be deleted because I am restricting the information to my uncle from Mississippi, not my uncle from Ohio or some other place.)

11. The phrase in this sentence could be either restrictive or nonrestrictive.

    The orchestra, playing patriotic music, captivated the audience. (If there is only one orchestra playing and if this orchestra happens to be playing patriotic music, then the sentence is correct with the commas.)

    The orchestra playing patriotic music captivated the audience. (Suppose many orchestras are playing. People are outside wandering from orchestra to orchestra. One is playing patriotic music, another is playing show tunes, another is playing classical pieces, and yet another is playing rock 'n roll. But the only one captivating the audience is the one playing patriotic music. In this case, the commas should be deleted.)

12. This novel, which is my favorite, has been on the best-seller list for months. (Because the writer uses the word *this*, the reader knows what novel is being discussed. The information in the clause is nonessential. The word *which* and the commas are correct.)

13. In 2001 the American Youth Philharmonic was led by Leonard Slatkin, conductor of the National Symphony Orchestra, in the Concert Hall at the Kennedy Center. (A comma needs to added after *Orchestra* because the phrase is nonessential and should be set off with two commas.)

14. They are, after all, expecting a good show for their money. (Because the phrase *after all* is nonessential, it should be set off with commas.)

15. A new hit television series on ABC on Sunday nights, a fast-paced drama, has helped lift the ratings of the network. (The phrase *a fast-paced drama* is nonessential information and should be set off with commas. Do not use a comma before *on ABC on Sunday nights* because the information is restrictive.)

# Commas in a Series and with Coordinate Adjectives

Our discussion of commas concludes with three areas: commas **in a series**, commas **with coordinate adjectives**, and **special problems** with commas.

**Use commas to separate words, phrases, and clauses in a series.** The comma before *and* in a series of three or more items is a matter of style. For example, the *United States Government Printing Office Style Manual* and *The Chicago Manual of Style* require the comma in a series of three or more items, but the *Associated Press Stylebook,* like most journalistic styles, does not use the comma in a series. In this module, and throughout this book, we will use the comma in a series. In fact, the following *true* story may convince you that using the comma in a series is definitely to your advantage.

As the story goes, an elderly fellow, who had lived a long, long happy life, left his estate to his three sons. His will states that his sons John, Joe and Jeff are to share his estate. Note that no series comma is after *Joe* and that the gentleman did not include the word *equally*. John decides that since his dad had not included the series comma, he meant for him to have 50 percent of the estate and for his two brothers to share the other 50 percent. So sure is John that he hires an attorney, and they go to court. And who do you think wins? You got it! John. So watch your commas, and watch your brothers.

Here are some examples of commas with a series.

- ❏ **Words:** The carpenter brought his wrenches, pliers, hammers, screwdrivers, and saws.

- ❏ **Phrases:** The apprentice's responsibilities include tightening nuts and bolts, measuring boards for the bookcase, and using the miter box to make perfect angle cuts.

- ❏ **Clauses:** The client was thrilled that the bookcase had built-in lights, that the hardware was hidden, and that the shelves were adjustable.

## Commas with Coordinate Adjectives

**Use a comma to separate coordinate adjectives.** Coordinate adjectives are two or more adjectives separately modifying the same noun. Coordinate adjectives are placed in front of the noun they modify. So, you ask, how do you know if the adjectives are coordinate? Do the following tests:

Reverse the two adjectives.

Place the word *and* between the two adjectives.

If the adjectives pass both tests, separate the adjectives with a comma. Do not use a comma to separate two side-by-side adjectives that are not coordinate.

Here are examples of coordinate adjectives.

- ❏ The *intelligent, creative* contractor attracted many clients.

    **Test 1:** The *creative, intelligent* contractor attracted many clients.

    **Test 2:** The *intelligent and creative* contractor attracted many clients.

The sentences still make sense, so the comma should be used between the two adjectives.

❒ The *dark, damp* basement was full of spiders and crickets.

**Test 1:** The *damp, dark* basement was full of spiders and crickets.

**Test 2:** The *dark and damp* basement was full of spiders and crickets.

The sentences still make sense, so the comma should be used between the two adjectives.

Here are examples of adjectives that are not coordinate.

❒ I need a *red ballpoint* pen.

**Test 1:** I need a *ballpoint, red* pen.

**Test 2:** I need a *red and ballpoint* pen.

The sentences make no sense. Because the adjective *red* modifies the noun phrase *ballpoint pen,* the comma should not be used between the two adjectives.

❒ The *recent weather* report is calling for snow.

**Test 1:** The *weather, recent* report is calling for snow.

**Test 2:** The *recent and weather* report is calling for snow.

The sentences make no sense in either test. Because the adjective *recent* modifies the noun phrase *weather report,* the comma should not be used between the two adjectives.

# Confidence Check

Insert or delete commas to conform with the rules for items in a series and for coordinate adjectives. Remember that our style in this book is to use the comma in a series. If the sentence is correct as written, write "Correct" next to it.

1. The candidates, their spouses, their children, and their supporters, were present at the rally today.

2. A demagogue appeals to the greed, fears and prejudices of the voters.

3. The line of power is passed from the President to the Vice President, from the Vice President to the Speaker of the House, from the Speaker to the president pro tempore of the Senate, from the president pro tempore to the Secretary of State and from the Secretary of State to the Secretary of the Treasury.

4. This plan affects a left-wing liberal advocating reform, a right-wing conservative opposing progress, or a moderate taking a middle-of-the-road position.

5. This does not mean that a coup d'état will occur, that civil disobedience will be encouraged or that executive privilege will be imposed.

6. He used his last, bargaining chip to try to get his bill passed.

7. I am a strong advocate of the two-party, political system.

8. I hoped that the tall, handsome politician was willing to hear my story.

9. The senator plans to wear his new gray flannel pin-striped suit to the presidential dinner.

10. The defeated, lame duck knew his power had been diminished.

# Confidence Check Answers

1.  The candidates, their spouses, their children, and their supporters were present at the rally today. (Delete the comma after *supporters* because a comma does not follow the last item in a series.)

2.  A demagogue appeals to the greed, fears, and prejudices of the voters. (Insert a comma before *and* because the series has three items.)

3.  The line of power is passed from the President to the Vice President, from the Vice President to the Speaker of the House, from the Speaker to the president pro tempore of the Senate, from the president pro tempore to the Secretary of State, and from the Secretary of State to the Secretary of the Treasury. (Insert a comma before *and* because the series has five items and our style requires it.)

4.  This plan affects a left-wing liberal advocating reform, a right-wing conservative opposing progress, or a moderate taking a middle-of-the-road position. (This sentence correctly places a comma before *or* because there are three items in the series.)

5.  This does not mean that a coup d'état will occur, that civil disobedience will be encouraged, or that executive privilege will be imposed. (A comma should be placed before *or* because there are three items in the series and our style requires it.)

6.  He used his last bargaining chip to try to get his bill passed. (No comma should be placed after *last* because the adjectives *last* and *bargaining* are not coordinate. Using the two tests, we could not say *bargaining last chip* or *last and bargaining chip*.)

7.  I am a strong advocate of the two-party political system. (No comma should be placed after *two-party* because the adjectives are not coordinate. The adjective *two-party* is modifying the noun phrase *political system*. Using the tests, we could not say *political two-party system* or *two-party and political system*.)

8.  I hoped that the tall, handsome politician was willing to hear my story. (This sentence is correct because the two adjectives *tall* and *handsome* are coordinate.)

9.  The senator plans to wear his new gray flannel pin-striped suit to the presidential dinner. (This sentence is correct because the adjectives *new*, *gray*, *flannel*, and *pinstriped* are not coordinate. Because order matters, no commas are used are not coordinate.)

10. The defeated lame duck knew his power had been diminished. (No comma should be placed after *defeated* because it is modifying the noun phrase *lame duck*. Using the test, we could not say *lame defeated duck* or *lame and defeated duck*.)

# Special Comma Problems

**Use your style book's preferred approach for the treatment of degrees and titles.** Usually degrees and titles are set off with commas, but Jr. and Sr. are not.

Here are examples of commas with degrees and titles.

❏ The consultant is Lisa Tyler, M.D., a well-known surgeon.

❏ Gregory Anders Jr. was appointed director of the graphics department.

**Place a comma before closing quotation marks.** This rule, which has no logical basis, is a well-accepted convention in American English. Even when the comma is not part of the quoted material, place the comma before the closing quotation marks. Follow the same rule with periods.

Here are examples of commas with closing quotation marks.

❏ "The new Mac is great for the graphics we want to develop," stated Ms. Blume.

❏ Please send me a copy of "Designing With Precision," a recent article in the magazine published by the American Institute of Architecture.

Two exceptions to this rule may apply: (1) in written directions for changes to documents and (2) in directions in a user manual.

❏ In draft two of the contract, delete "by May 15", but do not insert a new date. (The writer does not want the comma deleted.)

❏ Type "XYZ", and then enter the remainder of your data. (If the comma were placed inside the closing quotation mark, the user would incorrectly type the comma as part of the command.)

**With three-part dates, use a comma before and after the year.** With two-part dates, do not use any commas.

Here are examples of commas with three- and two-part dates.

❏ On March 25, 2017, he turned 50 years old.

❏ The magazine I need is dated June 2016.

**Use two commas to set off the state when both the city and state are used.**

Here are examples of commas with a city and a state.

❏ Mr. Gutierrez will arrive from Chicago, Illinois, on the 7:30 shuttle.

❏ My brother lived in Springfield, Ohio, before moving to Seattle, Washington, in 2015.

**When words are omitted from a sentence to avoid unnecessary repetition, use a comma to indicate the omission.**

Here are examples of commas with words omitted.

❏ Bernard Shamim completed two cases; Henry Wong, eight.

❏ I was counting on the sunshine; Eric, snow.

# Confidence Check

Correct the comma usage in the following sentences. If the sentence is correct as written, write "Correct" next to it.

1. Jonas Salk, M.D. changed American life in the 1950s when he created the polio vaccine.

2. My uncle was born in San Diego, California and spent most of his early years in California.

3. Her short story, "Tomorrow is Today", will be published in the local newspaper next month.

4. Presidents Jimmy Carter and George W. Bush, like Dwight Eisenhower before them, always pronounce "nu' clee-ar" as "nu' cu-lar", but they are unaware of their error.

5. The May 1, 2017 report claims that our agency will be over budget if we do not curtail spending immediately.

6. My nephew does not want to be known as George Wellington, Jr. because he wants his own identity.

7. The area around Riverside, California, has some of the most polluted air in the country.

8. At the restaurant Miguel ordered pasta; Simone, sirloin.

# Confidence Check Answers

1. Jonas Salk, M.D., changed American life in the 1950s when he created the polio vaccine. (A comma is needed before and after the degree.)

2. My uncle was born in San Diego, California, and spent most of his early years in California. (When a city and a state are used together, a comma is placed before and after the state.)

3. Her short story, "Tomorrow is Today," will be published in the local newspaper next month. (A comma is placed inside a closing quotation mark.)

4. Presidents Jimmy Carter and George W. Bush, like Dwight Eisenhower before them, always pronounced "nu' clee-ar" as "nu' cu-lar," but they were unaware of their error. (A comma is placed inside a closing quotation mark.)

5. The May 1, 2017, report claims that our agency will be over budget if we do not curtail spending immediately. (A comma is placed before and after the year in a three-part date.)

6. My nephew does not want to be known as George Wellington Jr. because he wants his own identity. (Commas are typically not used with Jr., but check your style guide.)

7. The area around Riverside, California, has some of the most polluted air in the country. (This sentence is correct because a comma is placed before and after a state name when both the city and state are written.)

8. At the restaurant Miguel ordered pasta; Simone, sirloin. (This sentence is correct because a comma is used to replace the missing word *ordered* after Simone.)

# Colons

A colon is a mark of introduction. The misuse of the colon is one of my pet peeves. The easiest thing to remember is that the colon must follow a complete sentence. The word group that follows the colon does not necessarily have to be a complete sentence, but the words that precede the colon do. The colon may be used to introduce the following:

**A quotation**

❑ Mr. Hart spoke earnestly with his staff: "If we are not frank with one another, we will conceal our mistakes rather than learn from them."

**A series or a list**

❑ The menu included a wide variety of dishes: flan, fajitas, quiche, and falafel.

**An independent clause that completes the meaning of the previous independent clause**

❑ We reached a conclusion: hard work is necessary to succeed. (Check your style manual to determine whether or not to capitalize the first letter of the first word of a complete sentence that follows a colon.)

A colon should not be used in the following instances:

**After *such as***

❑ Watch out for typographical errors, such as transposed letters, extra letters, or missing letters. (No colon should be placed after *such as* because the word group *Watch out for typographical errors, such as* is not a complete sentence. The comma is correctly placed after *errors* because the words after the comma are a nonrestrictive phrase.)

**Between a preposition and its object**

❑ The annual report consists of the introduction, the discussion, the recommendations, and the appendix. (No colon should follow the preposition *of* because the word group *The annual report consists of* is not a complete sentence.)

**Between a verb and its object**

❑ The accountant knew his assistant needed a new printer, a computer with more memory, a scanner, and updated word processing software. (No colon should follow the verb *needed* because the word group *The accountant knew his assistant needed* is not a complete sentence.)

# Confidence Check

Correct any colon errors in the following sentences. If a sentence is correct, write "Correct" next to it.

1. The areas we will study are: the skeletal system, circulatory system, muscular system, and nervous system.

2. The eye tests are for: cataracts, glaucoma, and astigmatism.

3. These expenses do not include the following annual fixed charges on plant cost: interest on debt, depreciation or amortization expenses, and taxes.

4. The annual report shows the historical plant cost of: selected hydroelectric, fossil-fuel-based steam-electric, gas-turbine, and nuclear steam-electric plants.

5. The prefatory material consists of three sections: the foreword, the introduction, and the highlights.

6. Follow these directions: take one pill before meals and two at bedtime.

7. We reached a conclusion: we need to cut down on our spending if we want to take a trip to France.

8. We completed the report by June 15: then we sent copies to the employees for their input.

9. Traveling to Manhattan is very expensive: a room in a moderately priced hotel costs over $300.

10. My office is on the fourth floor: his office is on the tenth.

# Confidence Check Answers

1. The areas we will study are the skeletal system, circulatory system, muscular system, and nervous system. (No colon should follow the verb *are* because the word group preceding the colon is not a complete sentence.)

2. The eye tests are for cataracts, glaucoma, and astigmatism. (No colon should follow the preposition *for* because the word group preceding the colon is not a complete sentence.)

3. These expenses do not include the following annual fixed charges on plant cost: interest on debt, depreciation or amortization expenses, and taxes. (The colon is used correctly in this sentence. The word group that precedes the colon is a complete sentence. Remember that the word group that follows a colon does not have to be a complete sentence.)

4. The annual report shows the historical plant cost of selected hydroelectric, fossil-fuel-based steam-electric, gas-turbine, and nuclear steam-electric plants. (No colon should follow the preposition *of* because the word group preceding the colon is not a complete sentence.)

5. The prefatory material consists of three sections: the foreword, the introduction, and the highlights. (The colon is used correctly in this sentence. The word group that precedes the colon is a complete sentence. Remember that the word group that follows a colon does not have to be a complete sentence.)

6. Follow these directions: take one pill before meals and two at bedtime. (The colon is used correctly in this sentence. The word group that precedes the colon is a complete sentence. The word group that follows the colon explains the previous sentence.)

7. We reached a conclusion: we need to cut down on our spending if we want to take a trip to France. (The colon is used correctly in this sentence. The word group that precedes the colon is a complete sentence. The word group that follows the colon explains the previous sentence.)

8. We completed the report by June 15; then we sent copies to the employees for their input. (Because the second sentence does not explain the previous sentence, the use of the colon is incorrect. The two independent clauses should be separated by a semicolon because the ideas are closely related. You might say that the second sentence actually continues the story rather than explains it. The clauses could, of course, be separated by a period.)

9. Traveling to Manhattan is very expensive: a room in a moderately priced hotel costs over $300. (This sentence could be correct as it stands because the sentence after the colon explains the previous one. However, one might say that the two independent clauses could be separated by a semicolon because the ideas are closely related and the second sentence continues the information in the first sentence. Either way would be acceptable. But no matter which punctuation point you choose, you should always be ready to verify what you have done.)

10. My office is on the fourth floor; his office is on the tenth. (Because the second sentence does not explain the previous one, the use of the colon is incorrect. The two independent clauses should be separated by a semicolon because the ideas are closely related. You might say that the second sentence continues the story rather than explains it.)

# Semicolons

**A semicolon should be used to separate two constructions of generally equal weight.** Remember, a semicolon is stronger than a comma, but weaker than a period. Generally, a semicolon is used to separate two independent clauses without a coordination or subordinating conjunction or with a conjunctive adverb.

❏ Proofreading requires alertness; a tired mind will miss many errors.

❏ She completed her report on time; however, she neglected to proofread it.

A semicolon should be used to separate items in a series when one or more of the items in the series contain commas.

❏ Seminars were conducted in Dallas, Texas, on July 18, 2017; in Washington, DC, on October 21, 2017; and in St. Louis, Missouri, on December 13, 2017.

A semicolon should be used to separate two independent clauses joined by a coordinating conjunction when at least one of the clauses contains commas that could result in a misreading of the sentence. This is an exception to the rule that the comma, not the semicolon, is used with coordinating conjunctions joining independent clauses. The coordinating conjunctions are *for, and, nor, but, or, yet,* and *so.*

❏ We ordered legal paper, toner cartridges, and black ballpoint pens; but manila folders, envelopes, and binder clips were sent instead.

# Confidence Check

Correct the punctuation in the following sentences.

1. We visited Madison, Wisconsin, on February 22, 2017, Tampa, Florida, on April 1, 2017, Pittsburgh, Pennsylvania, on June 3, 2017, and Toledo, Ohio, on July 1, 2017.

2. My favorite works of literature are *Leaves of Grass*, a collection of poetry by Walt Whitman, *The Glass Menagerie*, a play by Tennessee Williams, and *To Kill A Mockingbird*, a novel by Harper Lee.

3. We have confirmed our plans for our stay in Florence, however, our Venice plans are still in the planning process.

4. My daughter returned home three minutes after she left the house, she had forgotten her backpack.

5. He successfully completed courses in contracting procedures, stress management, and writing directives, and courses in report writing, oral presentations, and time management are on his training plan for next year.

6. My son was required to purchase insulated hiking boots, which he will need for mountain climbing, a 21-speed bike, which he will use for mountain biking, *Living with Nature*, a pamphlet that introduces him to the rigors of outdoor life, and a whistle, which is a safety necessity for all campers.

7. Many Americans view John F. Kennedy as rich, young, handsome, articulate, and intelligent, yet others believe him to be an ineffectual president, just as he was an ineffectual senator.

8. Chances are we are not as different as you think, we can learn a great deal from one another.

9. The forecasters predicted four inches of snow therefore the city had its snow plows ready and waiting.

10. I was invited to a cut-throat Scrabble game, a concert, and a Super Bowl party, but of course, in the end I stayed home to write a chapter of my book.

# Confidence Check Answers

1. We visited Madison, Wisconsin, on February 22, 2017; Tampa, Florida, on April 1, 2017; Pittsburgh, Pennsylvania, on June 3, 2017; and Toledo, Ohio, on July 1, 2017. (Because each item in the series has internal commas, each item should be followed by a semicolon, not a comma.)

2. My favorite works of literature are *Leaves of Grass*, a collection of poetry by Walt Whitman; *The Glass Menagerie*, a play by Tennessee Williams; and *To Kill A Mockingbird*, a novel by Harper Lee. (Because each item in the series has an internal comma, each item should be followed by a semicolon, not a comma.)

3. We have confirmed our plans for our stay in Florence; however, our Venice plans are still in the planning process. (Because this sentence is composed of two independent clauses joined by the conjunctive adverb *however*, a semicolon should precede the adverb.)

4. My daughter returned home three minutes after she left the house; she had forgotten her backpack. (Because this sentence is composed of two closely related independent clauses, they should be joined with a semicolon. Remember, a comma is not strong enough to be between two complete sentences.)

5. He successfully completed courses in contracting procedures, stress management, and writing directives; and courses in report writing, oral presentations, and time management are on his training plan for next year. (Usually a comma precedes a coordinating conjunction that joins two independent clauses; but since the clauses have internal commas, a semicolon should precede the coordinating conjunction *and* for clarity for the reader.)

6. My son was required to purchase insulated hiking boots, which he will need for mountain climbing; a 21-speed bike, which he will use for mountain biking; "Living With Nature," a pamphlet which will introduce him to the rigors of outdoor life; and a whistle, which is a safety necessity for all campers. (Because each item in the series has an internal comma, each item should be followed by a semicolon, not a comma.)

7. Many Americans view John F. Kennedy as rich, young, handsome, articulate, and intelligent; yet others believe him to be an ineffectual president, just as he was an ineffectual senator. (Usually a comma precedes a coordinating conjunction that joins two independent clauses; but because the clauses have internal commas, a semicolon should precede the coordinating conjunction *yet* for clarity for the reader.)

8. Chances are we are not as different as you think; we can a learn a great deal from one another. (Because this sentence is composed of two closely related independent clauses, they should be joined with a semicolon. Remember, a comma is not strong enough to be between two complete sentences.)

9. The forecasters predicted four inches of snow; therefore, the city had its snow plows ready and waiting. (Because this sentence is composed of two independent clauses joined by the conjunctive adverb *therefore*, a semicolon should precede the adverb.)

10. I was invited to a cut-throat Scrabble game, a concert, and a Super Bowl party; but of course, in the end I stayed home to write a chapter of my book. (Usually a comma precedes a coordinating conjunction that joins two independent clauses; but because the clauses have internal commas, a semicolon should precede the coordinating conjunction *but* for clarity for the reader.)

# Hyphens

Fay got beeped by call-waiting while she was talking on the telephone with a friend. Fay answered the call and said to her second friend, "I'll call you back; I'm on the other line with new minister gossip." In a few minutes, Fay returned the call to her second friend, who said, "I didn't know you guys were getting a new minister." To which Fay promptly replied, "We're not. We have new gossip about the minister."

We often punctuate with our voices. In writing, a hyphen can change the meaning of a phrase.

Notice the difference in the meaning of the following phrases:

❑ four-year-old children (a group of children; each child is four years old)

❑ four year-old children (four children; each child is one year old)

Would this difference in meaning be of interest to a childcare provider? You bet it would.

Hyphenation is probably one of the most confusing elements of style. Both *The Government Printing Office Style Manual* and *The Chicago Manual of Style* have endless rules for the hyphen. Be sure to check your style manual to verify each hyphen you choose to include or not to include. Although the rules vary significantly, we do have some universal guidelines. Always be sure to check your dictionary of choice, because this could override a general rule in your style manual. When a term in the dictionary is hyphenated, the term retains the hyphen, no matter where it "lives" in a sentence. Words such as time-consuming and cost-effective are often called permanent compounds.

In general, do not use a hyphen to set off a prefix at the beginning of a word.

❑ antiwar, anticult

❑ multipiece, multicolor

❑ semiannual, semigloss

❑ subdivision, subspecies

❑ reorganize, reattach

Whenever necessary, use a hyphen to avoid misunderstanding.

❑ re-cover (as a piece of furniture)

❑ recover (from an illness)

❑ un-ionize (opposite of ionize)

❑ unionize (to form a union)

To avoid misreading, use a hyphen after a prefix that ends with *a* or *i* when the root word begins with the same letter.

❑ ultra-active

❑ anti-intellectual

Do not use a hyphen when the prefix ends with *e* or *o* and the root word begins with the same letter. (This rule has some exceptions, such as *de-emphasize*.)

- ❏ reevaluate

- ❏ coordinate

When a prefix is added to a word that begins with a capital, use a hyphen after the prefix.

- ❏ mid-April

Hyphenate the elements of a unit modifier that occurs before a noun.

- ❏ an old-fashioned idea

- ❏ long-term loans

- ❏ flood-stricken area

- ❏ a law-abiding citizen

- ❏ a closed-door discussion

- ❏ a well-known author

- ❏ an 8-percent increase

These words are usually not hyphenated when they follow a verb.

- ❏ The loans are long term.

- ❏ The area was flood stricken.

- ❏ The citizen is law abiding.

However, dictionaries will let you know if a word is a permanent compound; that is, if it is always hyphenated, no matter where it is in a sentence. Always check your dictionary.

- ❏ The author is well-known.

- ❏ The walkie-talkie is the latest model.

Hyphenate phrases used as unit modifiers before a noun.

- ❏ a hard-and-fast rule

- ❏ a day-by-day account

A number of unit modifiers are actually well-established compound nouns serving as adjectives. These expressions refer to well-known concepts or institutions. Because they are easily grasped as a unit, do not use a hyphen.

- ❏ real estate agent

- ❏ social security tax

- ❏ civil rights case

Do not hyphenate compounds that end with the following words:

- ❒ -wide: worldwide, citywide, companywide, statewide

- ❒ -proof: waterproof, fireproof

- ❒ -worthy: newsworthy, trustworthy

- ❒ -long: lifelong, daylong

Do not hyphenate a unit modifier if the first word is an adverb ending in *-ly*.

- ❒ an eagerly awaited moment

- ❒ a quickly reviewed report

Do, however, hyphenate a unit modifier if the first word is an adjective ending in *-ly*.

- ❒ a friendly-looking dog

- ❒ a motherly-sounding woman

When two or more hyphenated adjectives have a common base word (usually a noun) and this word is shown only with the last term, insert a hyphen after each adjective. This is called a suspended hyphen.

- ❒ one- and two-semester courses

- ❒ two-, three-, and four-foot boards

If the terms are usually one word, then use the hyphen with the prefixes and close up the word with the common element.

- ❒ pre- and posttest

- ❒ light- and heavyweight fighters

Use a hyphen in place of the word *to* to link two figures that represent a continuous sequence.

- ❒ on pages 26-34

- ❒ during the years 2001-2016

Do not use the hyphen if the sequence is introduced by the word *from* or the word *between*.

- ❒ from 2001 to 2016

- ❒ between 2001 and 2016

Use a hyphen in fractions and compound numbers.

- ❒ one-half

- ❒ thirty-nine

# Confidence Check

Underline the correct form in each of the following pairs.

1.  nonabrasive                     non-abrasive

2.  unAmerican                      un-American

3.  recreation of the Battle of     re-creation of the Battle of
    Manassas                        Manassas

4.  a hit or miss plan              a hit-or-miss plan

5.  pre-World War I                 pre World War I

6.  hair-raising experience         hair raising experience

7.  email                           E-mail

8.  The organization was well       The organization was well-
    established.                    established.

9.  antiinstitutional               anti-institutional

10. highest ranking official        highest-ranking official

11. decentralize                    de-centralize

12. multiply                        multi-ply

13. long-lasting results            long lasting results

14. a statewide law                 a state-wide law

15. user-friendly software          user friendly software

16. a 30 year mortgage              a 30-year mortgage

17. re-establish                    reestablish

18. pretest                         pre-test

19. well-qualified applicant        well qualified applicant

20. a 90-degree angle               a 90 degree angle

21. rapidly rising prices           rapidly-rising prices

22. homely looking dog              homely-looking dog

23. a high-school student           a high school student

24. 3-, 4-, and 5-gallon            3, 4, and 5-gallon containers
    containers

25. from 2015-2020                  from 2015 to 2020

# Confidence Check Answers

1.  nonabrasive (Words beginning with the prefix *non-* should not be hyphenated.)

2.  un-American (A hyphen is used between a prefix and a proper noun because of the capital letter.)

3.  re-creation of the Battle of Manassas (To avoid confusion in meaning, the hyphen is needed.)

4.  a hit-or-miss plan (Phrases used as unit modifiers before a noun should be hyphenated.)

5.  pre-World War I (A hyphen is used between a prefix and a proper noun because of the capital letter.)

6.  hair-raising experience (A unit modifier before a noun is hyphenated.)

7.  Email, email, E-mail, and e-mail are all correct. (Check your organization's style preference.)

8.  The organization was well established. (Modifiers that follow a verb are usually not hyphenated.)

9.  anti-institutional (To avoid misreading, when a prefix ends with *a* or *i* and the root word begins with the same letter, a hyphen should be used.)

10. highest-ranking official (A unit modifier before a noun is hyphenated; however, be sure to check your style manual. Some styles do not hyphenate comparative and superlative adjectives.)

11. decentralize (Words beginning with the prefix *de-* are usually not hyphenated.)

12. Both are correct. The first one indicates a mathematics process; the second one means "many layers."

13. long-lasting results (A unit modifier before a noun is hyphenated.)

14. a statewide law (words ending with *-wide* should not be hyphenated.)

15. user-friendly software (A unit modifier before a noun is hyphenated.)

16. a 30-year mortgage (A unit modifier before a noun is hyphenated.)

17. reestablish (Words beginning with the prefix *re-* should not be hyphenated.)

18. pretest (Words beginning with the prefix *pre-* should not be hyphenated.)

19. well-qualified applicant (A unit modifier before a noun is hyphenated.)

20. a 90-degree angle (A unit modifier before a noun is hyphenated.)

21. rapidly rising prices (A hyphen should not follow an adverb that ends with *-ly*.)

22. homely-looking dog (An adjective ending with *–ly* is hyphenated when it is used as a unit modifier.)

23. a high school student (Clearly understood compounds need no hyphen.)

24. 3-, 4-, and 5-gallon containers (When two or more hyphenated adjectives have a common base word and this word is shown only with the last term, a hyphen should be placed after each adjective.)

25. from 2015 to 2020 (When the word *from* is used, the word *to* must be used.)

# Apostrophes

Apostrophes show omission as in contractions, such as *don't*, *isn't*, and *couldn't*; however, in formal writing, contractions should be avoided.

Apostrophes also show possession. For some reason, this use of the apostrophe is a thorn in everyone's side. It need not be. The easiest rule to remember is that if a noun ends in an "-s," just add an apostrophe to make it possessive. And if the noun does not end in an "-s," add an apostrophe and an "-s" to make it possessive. Although it is not necessary to be concerned about whether a word is singular or plural, the following chart may help you.

| Singular | Singular Possessive | Plural | Plural Possessive |
|---|---|---|---|
| girl | girl's hat | girls | girls' hats |
| man | man's hat | men | men's hats |
| boss | boss' hat* | bosses | bosses' hats |
| son-in-law | son-in-law's hat | sons-in-law | sons-in-law's hats |

\* Be sure to use your organization's style to form possessives of nouns. Some styles dictate that singular nouns that end in *-s* and produce another syllable require that an apostrophe and an *-s* be added.

Individual possession differs from joint possession. When two or more nouns possess another noun individually, each noun should show possession.

Here is an example of an **individual** possession:

❑ Kevin's and Terri's offices are being repainted. (In this example, Kevin and Terri have separate offices.)

When two or more nouns possess another noun jointly, only the last noun should show possession.

Here is an example of a **joint** possession:

❑ Kevin and Terri's office is being repainted. (In this example, Kevin and Terri share an office.)

Do not use apostrophes to form the possessive of pronouns. Remember, *it's* is a contraction for *it is*, but *its* is a possessive pronoun.

Check to see if your organizational style uses the apostrophe for the following situations:

❑ Plurals of letters: t's or ts.

❑ Plurals of decades and other figures: 1960's or 1960s; 2's or 2s

❑ Plurals of symbols and acronyms: RIF's or RIFs

❑ Omission in years: '14 or 2014

# Confidence Check

Change the incorrect use of apostrophes in the following sentences. If the apostrophe is used correctly in the sentence, write "Correct" next to it.

1. I thought the keys were her's.


2. This book is my daughter's.


3. My daughters-in-laws' ideas for the surprise party were terrific.


4. We have to be attuned to our childrens' needs.


5. Updating the 16 handbook is Chester and Tim's responsibility.


6. The preschool administrator wanted to know if my three-year-old nephew knows his ABCs.


7. Count the *and*'s in that paragraph.


8. The witness's testimony was struck from the records.

# Confidence Check Answers

1. I thought the keys were *hers*. (Possessive pronouns do not have apostrophes.)

2. This book is my *daughter's*. (Correct—A noun that does not end in an *s* is made possessive by adding an apostrophe and an *s*.)

3. My *daughters-in-law's* ideas for the surprise party were terrific. (Because the plural noun does not end in an *s*, an apostrophe and an *s* are added.)

4. We have to be attuned to our *children's* needs. (Because the plural noun does not end in an *s*, an apostrophe and an *s* are added.)

5. Updating the *'16* handbook is Chester and *Tim's* responsibility. (An apostrophe is needed before *16* to show omission, although writing the full year, 2016, might be a better correction; the apostrophe after *Tim* is correct because it indicates joint ownership.)

6. The preschool administrator wanted to know if my three-year-old nephew knows his *ABCs*. (Correct according to some styles; other styles may insert an apostrophe—*ABC's*. Be sure to check your style manual.)

7. Count the *and's* in that paragraph. (Correct according to some styles; other styles may omit the apostrophe [*and*s]. Be sure to check your style manual.)

8. The *witness'* testimony was struck from the records. (Since the noun already ends with an *s*, only an apostrophe needs to be added; however, adding the *s* may be correct according to some styles [witness's]. Be sure to check your style manual.)

# Quotation Marks

The rules for quotation marks can get a bit confusing because they are not related to logic in any way. My best advice is to always check the rule before using the quotation marks. Because we don't use them that often, these rules are not worth memorizing; however, they are worth looking up in a reference book. Put periods and commas inside the closing quotation marks. This is the American style. The American convention for placing commas and periods inside quotation marks offers no logic. If you deal with publications from England or Australia or South Africa, the rules for the quotation mark will differ.

Here are examples of a period and comma with quotation marks:

- ❏ The letter was marked "Confidential."

- ❏ She described her new friend as "tall," "handsome," and "intelligent."

Put colons and semicolons outside the closing quotation marks. Again there is no logic to this rule.

Here are examples of quotation marks with colons and semicolons:

- ❏ I had my doubts when I heard him say, "Your check is in the mail"; needless to say, I have received nothing.

- ❏ We know what she means when she says to use some "ingenuity": creativity wins proposals.

Use the following patterns for question marks and exclamation points at the end of a sentence concluding with a quotation:

Here are examples of quotation marks with question marks and exclamation points:

When the quote is not a question, but the sentence is.

- ❏ Did they say, "We'll help"?

When the quote is a question, but the sentence is not.

- ❏ They asked, "May we help?"

When the quote is a question, and so is the sentence.

- ❏ Did they ask, "May we help?"

When the quote is an exclamation, and the sentence is a question.

- ❏ Who yelled, "The sky is falling!"

When the quote is a question, and the sentence is an exclamation.

- ❏ Don't ask, "Where is the exit"!

Use quotation marks for a direct quote, not for an indirect quotation.

Here's a **direct quote**:

❒ The forerunner declared, "My political record shows that I am the best person for the job."

Here's an **indirect quote**:

❒ The forerunner declared that his political record shows that he is the best person for the job.

**Note:** Single quotes are treated the same way as double quotes.

# Confidence Check

Change the incorrect use of quotation marks in each of the following sentences. If the quotation marks are correct, write "Correct" next to the sentence.

1. Mrs. Ludsky asked "if she would be receiving a raise?"

2. The envelope was marked "Return to sender. Address unknown."

3. I just finished reading the article "Improve Your Health With Exercise".

4. Mrs. Moore said, "I just finished reading the article 'Improve Your Health With Exercise'."

5. Her latest article, "Success in the Millennium", appeared in *The Washington Post*.

6. He asked, "Would you like to travel with me to Europe?"

7. Did he ask, "Would you like to travel with me to Europe?"

8. Did he say, "I will buy you a first-class ticket to Europe"?

# Confidence Check Answers

1.  Mrs. Ludsky asked if she would be receiving a raise. (Quotation marks are not used with indirect quotes. The sentence should end with a period, not a question mark.)

2.  The envelope was marked "Return to sender. Address unknown." (This sentence is correct because periods are always placed inside quotation marks.)

3.  I just finished reading the article "Improve Your Health With Exercise." (Periods are always placed inside quotation marks.)

4.  Mrs. Moore said, "I just finished reading the article 'Improve Your Health With Exercise.'" (Periods are always placed inside single quotation marks as well as double quotation marks.)

5.  Her latest article, "Success in the Millennium," appeared in *The Washington Post*. (Commas are always placed inside quotation marks.)

6.  He asked, "Would you like to travel with me to Europe?" (Correct—Because the quoted information is a question and the entire sentence is a statement, the question mark has been correctly placed inside the quotation mark.)

7.  Did he ask, "Would you like to travel with me to Europe?" (Correct—Because the quoted information is a question and the entire sentence is a question, the question mark has been correctly placed inside the quotation mark.)

8.  Did he say, "I will buy you a first-class ticket to Europe"? (Correct—Because the quoted information is a statement and the entire sentence is a question, the question mark has been correctly placed outside the quotation mark.)

# Parentheses

Occasionally, you may want to insert words into a sentence that interrupt its normal word order. Parentheses de-emphasize information. They tell a reader, "You can skip this extra information if you want."

☐ Cyclamen (called the poor person's orchid) makes a good houseplant for cool rooms.

If the word group in parentheses occurs within the sentence, don't start the word group with a capital letter or end it with a period, even if it is a complete sentence.

☐ Brian's down jacket (he bought it last week) keeps him warm in Ithaca weather.

But if the word group is a question or an exclamation, place a question mark or exclamation point inside the parentheses.

☐ I thought the play (it was a comedy, wasn't it?) lacked a solid plot line.

If the material in parentheses is a complete sentence standing by itself, begin it with a capital letter and end it with a period inside the closing parentheses.

☐ We left San Francisco early. (It was just in time, too.) The earthquake hit soon after ten o'clock.

When parentheses are used at the end of a sentence, the parenthetical material may be treated as part of the sentence or as a separate sentence. Note the differences in capitalization and the position of the period.

☐ This issue is discussed in chapter 10 (see pages 92-99).

☐ This issue is discussed in chapter 10. (See pages 92-99.)

When using parentheses to list items in a series in running text, be sure to use both the opening and closing parentheses, not just the closing.

☐ Her spring was filled with many activities: (1) volunteering as president of the garden club, (2) participating in the neighborhood clean-up campaign, and (3) jogging five miles a day.

# Confidence Check

Change the incorrect use of parentheses in the following sentences. If the parentheses are used correctly, write "Correct" next to the sentence.

1.  Our accountant cannot address this problem (She will be in Ohio until the end of the month), but perhaps I can help you.

2.  You may participate in our easy payment plan to finance your new car. (For more information, see the enclosed brochure.)

3.  He immediately tried to do three things: 1) call Ms. Yeger, 2) contact our regional office, and 3) alert the human relations office to the problem.

4.  To determine your eligibility, refer to the chart of academic credits (see page 216.)

5.  Mr. Young left early to testify (the court was to convene at 10 a.m.).

# Confidence Check Answers

1. Our accountant cannot address this problem (she will be in Ohio until the end of the month), but perhaps I can help you. (The sentence in the parentheses should not begin with a capital letter because it is embedded in another sentence.)

2. You may participate in our easy payment plan to finance your new car. (For more information, see the enclosed brochure.) (Correct—Because the sentence in parentheses stands by itself, it begins with a capital letter and ends with a period.)

3. He immediately tried to do three things: (1) call Ms. Yeger, (2) contact our regional office, and (3) alert the human relations office to the problem. (Parentheses come in pairs.)

4. To determine your eligibility, refer to the chart of academic credits (see page 216). (Because the information in the parentheses is embedded in the previous sentence, the period should follow the closing parenthesis. The sentence could also have been punctuated as follows: To determine your eligibility, refer to the chart of academic credits. (See page 216.)

5. Mr. Young left early to testify (the court was to convene at 10 a.m.). (Correct—Because the information in the parentheses is embedded in the previous sentence, the period should follow the closing parenthesis. The sentence could also have been punctuated as follows: Mr. Young left early to testify. (The court was to convene at 10 a.m.)

# Ellipses, Dashes, and Brackets

## Ellipses

If one or more words are omitted from the beginning or middle of a direct quote, use an ellipsis to indicate the omission. If one or more words are omitted at the end of a direct quote, use the ellipsis and then the necessary terminal punctuation for the entire sentence.

❏ "During the Persian Gulf Crisis...many nations joined forces to resolve the conflict."

❏ "Consumers adjust their buying habits when the nation sinks into a recession...."

## Dashes

Use dashes to indicate greater separation than commas but less than parentheses. Dashes shout at a reader "Read this!" They have the opposite effect of parentheses. Use dashes instead of commas if commas already exist in the nonessential information.

❏ Muhammad Ali—star of talk shows, amateur poet, heavyweight champ— has written his autobiography.

Use a single dash to emphasize an added comment.

❏ Kyle could win a gold medal—provided he stays at 126 pounds.

If the interrupting word group is a statement, no period is needed inside the dashes. But if it is a question or an exclamation, you must add a question mark or an exclamation point before the second dash.

❏ The star of the new Broadway show—can you believe he's over 80?—shuns publicity and leads a quiet life.

## Brackets

Brackets are usually used to clarify something in a direct quote. They tell the reader that this information was not part of the original quote. Parentheses should not be used because parentheses could have been in the original quote.

❏ "He [Jackie Robinson] was elected to the Baseball Hall of Fame in 1962."

# Confidence Check

Change the incorrect use of ellipses, dashes, and brackets in the following sentences. If the punctuation is correct, write "Correct" next to the sentence.

1. Our entire staff—Meryl, George, Jeff, and Stan was out with the flu last week.

2. She makes the plans—I do the work!

3. Life, liberty, and the pursuit of happiness—these are the rights of American citizens.

4. The new employees will meet in Gavin Hall—the large, spacious new auditorium in the east wing of the convention center.

5. We all had one wish—a very important one, that the new year would bring peace to the world.

6. "In my lifetime we have had only...two, two-term presidents," stated the senator.

7. The candidate said, "We must improve the health care opportunities in this country...."

8. According to *The New York Times*, "The verdict of the jury (conviction on seven counts) was greeted with cheers and tears in the courtroom."

# Confidence Check Answers

1. Our entire staff—Meryl, George, Jeff, and Stan—was out with the flu last week. (Dashes come in pairs. A dash is needed before and after the information that is being emphasized.)

2. She makes the plans—I do the work! (Correct—A single dash is used to emphasize an added comment at the end of a sentence.)

3. Life, liberty, and the pursuit of happiness—these are the rights of American citizens. (Correct—The dash emphasizes the list at the beginning of the sentence.)

4. The new employees will meet in Gavin Hall—the large spacious, new auditorium in the east wing of the convention center. (Correct—Because a comma is in the nonessential information, a dash is needed for clarity.)

5. We all had one wish—a very important one—that the new year would bring peace to the world. (Dashes come in pairs. A dash is needed before and after the information that is being emphasized.)

6. "In my lifetime we have had only...two, two-term presidents," stated the senator. (Correct—An ellipsis is used to indicate that information has been omitted from a direct quote.)

7. The candidate said, "We must improve the health care opportunities in this country...." (Correct—At the end of a sentence, four dots are used, three for the ellipsis for the missing words and one for the terminal punctuation.)

8. According to *The New York Times*, "The verdict of the jury [conviction on seven counts] was greeted with cheers and tears in the courtroom." (Brackets should be used to add clarifying information to a quote.)

# Notes

# Module 4: Verb Tense, Mood, and Voice

## Verbs

Verbs are the power of the language. They are the words that spin the tales that we want to read as we're walking through the airport. Think of the different images you get in the following sentences:

- ☐ I walked down the hall.

- ☐ I ambled down the hall.

- ☐ I sped down the hall.

- ☐ I tripped down the hall.

- ☐ I stumbled down the hall.

- ☐ I pranced down the hall.

- ☐ I sauntered down the hall.

Verbs also have the power because they have tenses. The word *tense* means time. By changing the tense of a verb you can let your reader know *when* something is happening.

# The 12 Verb Tenses

You'll live a long, happy life if you can't name the 12 verb tenses. If I were to ask you to give me a sentence using the future perfect progressive tense, you might panic. Don't. You use the tense all the time. Notice the following example:

☐ By next week I **will have been editing** this document for three weeks.

| Simple Tenses | Singular | Plural |
|---|---|---|
| *Present* | | |
| 1st person | I walk | we walk |
| 2nd person | you walk | you walk |
| 3rd person | he/she/it walks | they walk |
| *Past* | | |
| 1st person | I walked | we walked |
| 2nd person | you walked | you walked |
| 3rd person | he/she/it walked | they walked |
| *Future* | | |
| 1st person | I will walk | we will walk |
| 2nd person | you will walk | you will walk |
| 3rd person | he/she/it will walk | they will walk |

| Perfect Tenses | Singular | Plural |
|---|---|---|
| *Present Perfect* | | |
| 1st person | I have walked | we have walked |
| 2nd person | you have walked | you have walked |
| 3rd person | he/she/it has walked | they have walked |
| *Past Perfect* | | |
| 1st person | I had walked | we had walked |
| 2nd person | you had walked | you had walked |
| 3rd person | he/she/it had walked | they had walked |
| *Future Perfect* | | |
| 1st person | I will have walked | we will have walked |
| 2nd person | you will have walked | you will have walked |
| 3rd person | he/she/it will have walked | they will have walked |

| **Progressive Tenses** | **Singular** | **Plural** |
|---|---|---|
| *Present Progressive* | | |
| 1st person | I am walking | we are walking |
| 2nd person | you are walking | you are walking |
| 3rd person | he/she/it is walking | they are walking |
| *Past Progressive* | | |
| 1st person | I was walking | we were walking |
| 2nd person | you were walking | you were walking |
| 3rd person | he/she/it was walking | they were walking |
| *Future Progressive* | | |
| 1st person | I will be walking | we will be walking |
| 2nd person | you will be walking | you will be walking |
| 3rd person | he/she/it will be walking | they will be walking |

| **Perfect Progressive Tenses** | **Singular** | **Plural** |
|---|---|---|
| *Present Perfect Progressive* | | |
| 1st person | I have been walking | we have been walking |
| 2nd person | you have been walking | you have been walking |
| 3rd person | he/she/it has been walking | they have been walking |
| *Past Perfect Progressive* | | |
| 1st person | I had been walking | we had been walking |
| 2nd person | you had been walking | you had been walking |
| 3rd person | he/she/it had been walking | they had been walking |
| *Future Perfect Progressive* | | |
| 1st person | I will have been walking | we will have been walking |
| 2nd person | you will have been walking | you will have been walking |
| 3rd person | he/she/it will have been walking | they will have been walking |

# Mixing and Matching Tenses

In elementary and middle school you were probably taught to never mix your tenses. However, mixing tenses is actually not a problem. If I write you a letter and tell you what I did on a project last week, what I am doing on it today, and what I plan to do on it next week, I will most certainly mix my tenses.

Use the present tense to show a habitual present action; to express a universal truth; and to discuss literature, articles, and films.

❏ The book club meets the first Tuesday of each month.

❏ Water freezes (not froze) at 0° centigrade.

❏ The article explains the dangers of second-hand smoke.

Use the past tense to show a completed past action.

❏ I described the project to the committee.

Use the future tense to show future action.

❏ His partner will arrive this morning.

Use the present perfect tense to show a habitual past action or an action that started in the past and continues to the present.

❏ He has walked to work every day this week.

❏ We have worked here for six years.

Use the past perfect to express a past action that occurred before another past action.

❏ I hired Eva because she had worked in Europe for several years.

Use the future perfect to show a future action completed at a specific future time.

❏ By next week I will have jogged 100 miles.

Use the same tense to express two or more actions occurring in the same time frame.

❏ Although I said no, he insisted upon leaving immediately.

Use *will* to indicate simple future action; use *shall* to indicate mandatory future action.

❏ I understand that you will attend the meeting next Monday.

❏ Under the terms of your contract, you shall attend the weekly staff meeting.

Sometimes a helping verb or a main verb can be omitted in a compound verb.

❏ I have completed and mailed the application. (The helping verb *have* is understood before the main verb *mailed*. There is no need to repeat the helping verb.)

❏ I can and will maintain a chronological journal that will be available to the public. (The main verb *maintain* is understood after the helping verb *can*. There is no need to repeat the main verb.)

If the main verbs or the helping verbs are not the same, then the proper form must be used in each part of the compound verb.

❑ He never has forgotten and never will forget what the police force has done for him. (Notice the forms of the main verb and the helping verbs are different. Be sure to avoid the following error: He never has and never will forget what the police force has done for him. As this sentence stands, it means that he "never has forget," which does not make sense.)

Verbs have four principal parts. Be careful of irregular verbs.

❑ Present Tense: drink (s)

❑ Past Tense: drank

❑ Past Participle: drunk

❑ Present Participle: drinking

# Confidence Check

Correct the verb form in each of the following sentences. If the sentence is correct, write "Correct."

1.  I didn't know that Tallahassee was the capital of Florida.

2.  The article states that potatoes were not fattening.

3.  Ms. Krauss declined the job and then changed her mind.

4.  The supervisor walked into the room, sat at my desk, and begins checking his email without saying a word to anyone.

5.  The bright-eyed, young reporter for *The Washington Post* eyes the candidate, juts out his chin defiantly, and asked, "Why did you accept the $50,000 donation?"

6.  The California company hired Jeff because he lived in Argentina for many years.

7.  The meeting was canceled because adequate arrangements were not made.

8.  Marshall has an account in that bank for only six months.

9.  Frank worked here for seven years, but he plans to retire this summer.

10. George has been in my carpool until he moved to Ohio.

11. The regulations for Federal employees state that "No Federal employee will accept meals or gifts from a contractor."

12. We have and still are requesting a complete report on our trip to Japan.

# Confidence Check Answers

1. I didn't know that Tallahassee *is* the capital of Florida. (The present tense must be used as this is a general truth. If the verb *was* were left, the sentence would mean that Tallahassee is no longer the capital of Florida.)

2. The article states that potatoes *are* not fattening. (The present tense must be used as this is a general truth. If the verb *were* were left, the sentence would mean that potatoes used to be fattening, but they are not now.)

3. Ms. Krauss declined the job and then changed her mind. (Correct: Both verbs are in the past tense as they both occur in the same time frame.)

4. The supervisor walked into the room, sat at my desk, and *began* checking his email without saying a word to anyone. (All three verbs describe past actions.)

5. The bright-eyed, young reporter for *The Washington Post* eyes the candidate, juts out his chin defiantly, and *asks*, "Why did you accept the $50,000 donation?" (All three verbs should be in the same tense because they occur in the same time frame. Since the first two verbs are in the present tense, the third verb should also be in the present tense. Conceivably, all the verbs could be in the past tense.)

6. The California company hired Jeff because he *had* lived in Argentina for many years. (The past perfect is needed in the second verb because the living occurred before the hiring. One past action happened before another past action. If both verbs were left in the past tense, Jeff would be commuting from Argentina to California.)

7. The meeting was cancelled because adequate arrangements *had not been made*. (The past perfect is needed in the second verb because the not making occurred before the canceling. One past action happened before another past action.)

8. Marshall *has had* an account in that bank for only six months. (The present perfect tense is needed because the action of having started in the past but is still going on in the present.)

9. Frank *has worked* here for seven years, but he plans to retire this summer. (The present perfect tense is needed because the action started in the past but is still going on in the present.)

10. George *was* (or *had been*) in my carpool until he moved to Ohio. (The past tense is used for an action that occurred in the past. Since George is no longer in my carpool, the action is completed.)

11. The regulations for Federal employees state that "No Federal employee *shall* accept meals or gifts from a contractor." (Mandatory statements use *shall*.)

12. We have *requested* and still are requesting a complete report on our trip to Japan. (Since the form of the main verb is not the same, the verb must be written in its correct form; otherwise, the sentence would mean the following: We have requesting….)

# Mood

We have three moods in English: indicative, imperative, and subjunctive. Two of them, the indicative and the imperative, give us no problem. The third, the subjunctive, can often be a thorn in our side. Yes, the subjunctive is alive and well, although we don't see it in business writing that often.

The **indicative** mood is used to state a fact, ask a question, or give an opinion.

- ❏ The polls close at 7:00 p.m. (fact)

- ❏ When does your plane arrive? (question)

- ❏ Paris is the most beautiful city in the world. (opinion)

The **imperative** is used to express a command or make a request. In imperative sentences, the subject, you, is understood.

- ❏ Call me when you arrive home.

- ❏ Please send me a copy of your contract.

The **subjunctive** is used in dependent clauses that follow verbs of necessity, request, demand, or wishing. In the subjunctive, the present-tense verb is in the plural form with all subjects or the word *be* is used before the past participle. In addition, *were* is the only past tense form of *be*; *was* is never used.

- ❏ I demand that we be heard.

- ❏ We recommend that she be appointed to the committee.

- ❏ I wish I were going to Italy.

To express past time in a dependent clause that follows the verb *wish* use the past perfect tense.

- ❏ I wish that I had been accepted to the college of my choice.

The subjunctive is also used in *if, as if,* and *as though* clauses that state conditions that are improbable, doubtful, or contrary to fact. Be careful, not all *if* clauses are subjunctive.

- ❏ If I were you, I would accept the job. (This is contrary to fact. I will never be you.)

- ❏ If he were appointed (but he wasn't) head of the department, I would quit. (By using the subjunctive, the writer is stating that he will never be appointed head of the department.)

- ❏ If he is appointed head (he could be) of the department, I will quit. (In this sentence, the writer is indicating that there is a chance that he will be appointed head of the department.)

# Confidence Check

Use the correct verb form in each of the following sentences.

1. They suggested that he (change, changes) his plans.

2. Katie requested that Matt (inform, informs) her of his decision by the end of the week.

3. He demanded that we (are, be) on time.

4. I insisted that he (submit, submits) the proposal to the chairperson.

5. He requested that he (is told, be told, should be told) the results as soon as the tallying was complete.

6. It is important that she (calls, call) the office by noon.

7. My supervisor is busy now, but if she (wasn't, weren't), she would advise us.

8. I wish he (was, were) here today.

9. I wish José (had attended, attended) the meeting.

10. I move that Denise (is, be) appointed chairperson.

# Confidence Check Answers

All verbs in the sentences require the subjunctive.

1. They suggested that he *change* his plans.
2. Katie requested that Matt *inform* her of his decision by the end of the week.
3. He demanded that we *be* on time.
4. I insisted that he *submit* the proposal to the chairperson.
5. He requested that he *be told* the results as soon as the tallying was complete.
6. It is important that she *call* the office by noon.
7. My supervisor is busy now, but if she *weren't*, she would advise us.
8. I wish he *were* here today.
9. I wish José *had attended* the meeting.
10. I move that Denise *be* appointed chairperson.

# Confidence Check

*Underline each verb in the following paragraphs. Correct the verbs that are incorrect.*

To: Director, Fly-By-Night Travel Agency

From: Rita Woods

Subject: Travel Arrangements

I have encounter several problems on my past two trips arranged by the Fly-By-Night Travel Agency. For both trips, boarding passes were not attached for the Delta Airlines portion of my flight itinerary. Because my schedule was very tight on these trips, it is very important to have these boarding passes in advance.

In addition, the flight number for my second trip has been incorrect; this error caused further confusion and delay at the airport. To further complicate matters, the Fly-By-Night Travel Agency did not note the correct arrival time for the second flight. Thus, by the time I arrived in San Diego, my contact left the airport. As a result, I had no transportation to the conference.

I strongly recommend that your agents are reminded of the importance of accuracy and completeness when making travel arrangements for clients. I also suggest that each agent attends a proofreading workshop to improve visual acuity. Finally, I suggest that a supervisor check flight itineraries until the accuracy rate improves. Travel coordinators should be asked how they would feel if their travel was complicated by confusing plans.

# Possible Confidence Check Answers

To: Director, Fly-By-Night Travel Agency

From: Rita Woods

Subject: Travel Arrangements

I *encountered* several problems on my past two trips arranged by the Fly-By-Night Travel Agency. For both trips, boarding passes were not attached for the Delta Airlines portion of my flight itinerary. Because my schedule was very tight on these trips, it *was* very important to have these boarding passes in advance.

In addition, the flight number for my second trip *was* incorrect; this error caused further confusion and delay at the airport. To further complicate matters, the Fly-By-Night Travel Agency did not note the correct arrival time for the second flight. Thus, by the time I arrived in San Diego, my contact *had left* the airport. As a result, I had no transportation to the conference.

I strongly recommend that your agents *be* reminded of the importance of accuracy and completeness when making travel arrangements for clients. I also suggest that each agent *attend* a proofreading workshop to improve visual acuity. Finally, I suggest that a supervisor check flight itineraries until the accuracy rate improves. Travel coordinators should be asked how they would feel if their travel *were* complicated by confusing plans.

# Voice

The **voice** of a verb tells whether the subject of the sentence performs the action or is acted upon.

❑ *Henry shoveled* several driveways. (The subject acts.)

❑ Several *driveways were shoveled* by Henry. (The subject is acted upon; it is the object of the action verb *shovel*.)

Verbs whose subjects perform the action are in the **active voice**. Verbs whose subjects are acted upon are in the **passive voice**. The actor in a passive sentence may be named in a prepositional phrase or the actor may not be named at all.

❑ Several *driveways were shoveled*.

Passive verbs always consist of a form of *be* and the past participle of the main verb: *were shoveled, are torn, was named*. Other helping verbs may also be present: *have been shoveled, had been torn, would have been named*.

**Converting active to passive**

A sentence can be changed from active to passive voice by making the object of the verb the subject of the sentence and using the appropriate verb form.

**Converting passive to active**

A sentence can be changed from passive to active voice by making the actor of the verb the subject of the sentence. If the actor is unknown, the writer may have to create one. The subject of the passive sentence becomes the object of the active sentence.

Generally, writers should use the active voice because it gives more vigor to a manuscript. However, the use of the passive is legitimate, especially if the actor is either unknown or unimportant. Often, the passive can be droning.

# Confidence Check

Change passive voice verbs to active voice.

1. He lifted the cage door, and a hungry mouse was seen.

2. The proposal was submitted to the Planning Commission by Dr. Hendrick.

3. A study of the three available blood-testing systems was approved by the panel.

4. The time cards are prepared by the secretary by using the daily sign-in sheets.

5. Not before the opinion poll responses have been tabulated will it be possible to know if employees support the change.

6. Internal procedural manuals should be studied, and full use should be made of available reports.

7. The procedures adopted to carry out the hospital accreditation policy should be reviewed, progress reports should be examined, and it should be determined if our field examiners are complying with the prescribed policy.

8. We recommend that the college grant program be discontinued and current recipients, recent grant applicants, and all participating colleges be notified by the agency.

9. Consideration was being given to this matter by our executive officer.

10. It is desired by Mr. Brown that I call this to your attention.

11. An abstract should be prepared by an employee not connected with the billing or collection procedures for later comparison with the receipts issued.

12. Correspondence was seldom ordered reviewed by the director.

# Possible Confidence Check Answers

1. He lifted the cage door and saw a hungry mouse.

2. Dr. Hendrick submitted the proposal to the Planning Commission.

3. The panel approved a study of the three available blood-testing systems.

4. By using the daily sign-in sheets, the secretary prepares the time cards.

5. We must tabulate the opinion poll responses before we can know if employees support the change.

6. Study internal procedural manuals, and fully use available reports.

7. Review the procedures adopted to carry out the hospital accreditation policy, examine progress reports, and determine if our field examiners are complying with the prescribed policy.

8. We recommend that the agency discontinue the college grant program and notify current recipients, recent grant applicants, and all participating colleges.

9. Our executive officer considered this matter.

10. Mr. Brown wants me to call this to your attention.

11. An employee not connected with the billing or collection procedures should prepare an abstract for later comparison with the issued receipts.

12. The director seldom ordered that we review correspondence.

# Notes

# Module 5: Subject–Verb Agreement

## Subject–Verb Agreement

In theory, subject–verb agreement is quite simple: if the subject is singular, the verb is singular; if the subject is plural, the verb is plural. In reality, subject–verb agreement is one of the most common problems encountered by "word" people. Keep in mind that, physically, singular and plural nouns look the opposite of verbs. That is, singular nouns usually do not end with an *s*; singular verbs do, and plural nouns usually do end with an *s*; plural verbs do not. Notice the endings on the subjects and verbs in the following two examples:

❑ **Singular:** The boy walks to school every day.

❑ **Plural:** The boys walk to school every day.

When two or more subjects are joined by *and,* use a plural verb.

❑ The **editor** and the **proofreader need** a style manual.

But if these two or more subjects are preceded by the words *each* or *every* or joined anything other than *and,* use a singular verb.

❑ **Each editor** and **proofreader needs** a style manual.

❑ The **editor** as well as the proofreader **needs** a style manual.

Remember that *as well as, together with,* and *along with* do not have the force of the connective *and* and do not create a plural subject.

When two or more subjects are joined by the connectives *either/or, neither/nor, nor,* or *or*, make the verb agree with the subject that is closer to the verb.

❑ Either a new computer or a new **printer is needed.**

❑ Either my assistants or **Carrie Ogden is coordinating** conference arrangements.

❑ Either Carrie Ogden or my **assistants are coordinating** conference arrangements.

When the subject and verb are separated by intervening words, be sure to make the verb agree with the subject, not the intervening words.

❑ Just one **error** in all those values significantly **distorts** the result.

❑ **Paul**, along with the council members, **attends** every function.

❑ The **dictionary**, as well as the almanac, **is** a vital reference tool.

❑ **Either** of the proposals **is** acceptable to me.

❑ **Each** of the books **is** available in the library.

❑ **Neither** of the alternatives **is** feasible.

In the last three examples prepositional phrases modify the subjects. An object of a preposition can never be the subject of a sentence.

The following pronouns are considered singular and always require singular verbs. (Pronouns that refer to these indefinite pronouns must also be singular pronouns. We will discuss this in a later module.)

| | | |
|---|---|---|
| anybody | everyone | nothing |
| anyone | everything | one |
| each | neither | somebody |
| either | nobody | someone |
| everybody | no one | something |

Notice the words *either* and *neither* are on this list. Be careful when you see these words because they have three functions in the language. When they appear as the pairs (correlative conjunctions) *either...or* and *neither...nor*, they are connecting two subjects. When they appear alone as the subject of a sentence, they are pronouns and are always singular. When they appear before a noun, they are adjectives.

The following pronouns can be either singular or plural depending upon their use in a sentence: *some, most, all, which, that, who.* If the reference word (antecedent) is singular or is functioning as one unit, the pronoun is singular. If the antecedent is plural or is functioning as multiple entities, the pronoun is plural. Trust yourself on these words. While sound is not a rule, you will "hear" the correct verb for these pronouns. Although the object of the preposition can never be the subject of the sentence, it is often the word that lets you know whether the subject is singular or plural.

❏ **Some** of the cookies **were eaten** by the hungry boys, and **all** of the apples **have disappeared.** (*Some* is the subject of the first independent clause and refers to *cookies*; *all* is the subject of the second independent clause refers to *apples.* Therefore, both verbs are plural because the reference words are plural.)

❏ **Some** of the cookie **remains,** but **all** of the apple **was consumed.** (*Some* is the subject of the first independent clause and refers to *cookie*; *all* is the subject of the second independent clause and refers to *apple.* Therefore, both verbs are singular because the reference words are singular.)

If I were to ask you if the pronouns *who, that,* and *which* are singular or plural, the answer would be "both." When *who, that,* or *which* is the subject of a dependent clause, the antecedent (reference word) to the pronoun determines the number (singular or plural) of the verb. Remember, although a subject can never be in a prepositional phrase, an antecedent can.

❏ Chester is the videographer **who was invited** to make a presentation at the conference. (The pronoun *who* refers to the noun *videographer,* which is singular; therefore, the verb *was* is singular.)

❏ Chester is one of the videographers **who were invited** to make a presentation at the conference. (The pronoun *who* refers to the noun *videographers,* which is plural; therefore, the verb *were* is plural.)

Always think about the meaning of the sentence. In the first example (Chester is the videographer...), the writer is talking about one videographer. In the second example, the writer is talking about many videographers. (You can mentally rearrange the words to help you: Of the videographers who were invited....)

When the words *the only* are inserted before *one,* the antecedent of the pronoun is *one.*

❏ Chester is **the only one** of the videographers **who was** invited to make a presentation at the conference. (The pronoun *who* refers to the pronoun *one,* which is singular; therefore, the verb *was* is singular.)

Percentages and fractions functioning as subjects can be either singular or plural depending upon their use in a sentence. If the antecedent is singular or is functioning as a unit, the percentage or fraction is singular. If the antecedent is plural or is functioning as multiple entities, treat the percentage or fraction as plural. Again, the words in the prepositional phrase will help you determine the verb. Trust yourself!

- ❑ **Three-quarters** of the letters **have been typed**. (*Three-quarters* refers to the noun *letters*, which is plural; therefore, the verb *have* is plural.)

- ❑ **Three-quarters** of the letter **has been typed**. (*Three-quarters* refers to the noun *letter*, which is singular; therefore, the verb *has* is singular.)

- ❑ **Ninety percent** of the companies **have responded** to the survey. (*Ninety percent* refers to the noun *companies*, which is plural; therefore, the verb *have* is plural.)

- ❑ **Ninety percent** of the company **is owned** by the family. (*Ninety percent* refers to the noun *company*, which is singular; therefore, the verb *is* is singular.)

Amounts of time and money are usually considered a single unit and take a singular verb.

- ❑ The bank said that **$5,000 is needed** as collateral.

- ❑ **Fifty minutes is** not long enough to discuss the issue.

Collective nouns usually take a singular verb because the collective is usually thought of as a unit, not as individual members. A collective noun names a group of people or things that functions together as one unit. The following words are examples of collectives:

| | | |
|---|---|---|
| audience | crowd | group |
| class | department | jury |
| committee | division | mass |
| community | faculty | staff |
| company | family | team |

❏ The **audience was applauding** the swing dancers.

❏ The **committee has issued** its final report. (Note the use of the singular pronoun *its* to refer to the collective *committee*.)

Sometimes, the members of the collective may be viewed as individuals rather than as a group. In those instances, use a plural verb.

❏ The **faculty have received** their individual assignments for next month. (You can recast the sentence to read as follows: The **members** of the faculty **have received**....)

Remember, once you have made a sentence grammatically correct, look at it again. Is there a better way to write that sentence? I can stamp my feet all day long and even prove that *the faculty have* is grammatically correct. But if I have annoyed my reader, I will have accomplished nothing.

Words ending in *–ics,* such as *economics*, *acoustics*, and *statistics*, can be either singular or plural. Again, you can trust your ear. When these words refer to one course of study, they are singular; when they refer to qualities or activities, they are plural.

❏ **Statistics is** the class that most students dread.

❏ The **statistics prove** that consumers are happy with the new product.

Foreign plurals, such as *crises*, *analyses*, *media*, and *phenomena* (the singulars are *crisis*, *analysis*, *medium*, and *phenomenon*) require a plural verb. Some journalistic styles consider these words singular. However, strict grammarians regard them as the plurals that they are.

❏ The **media are** misleading the voters with inaccurate information.

❏ The **crises are** being discussed in every office.

Sometimes a subject will follow a verb. In such inverted sentences, be sure to identify the subject before selecting the form of the verb.

❏ There **are** a **candy bar** and a **balloon** for each child.

❏ **Enclosed are** the **documents** you need.

When functioning as subjects of a sentence, phrases and clauses are usually singular.

❑ **Participating in the Marine Corps marathon has** been her lifelong dream.

❑ **Whatever I say goes** in one ear and out the other.

But clauses beginning with *what* may be singular or plural. Check the word or words that follow the verb.

❑ **What he wants is** a new car.

❑ **What he wants are** new tires.

# Confidence Check

Underline the subject of each sentence. Then choose the correct verb in the parentheses.

1. Both José and Martha (is, are) on vacation this week.

2. Every student and parent (has, have) received a copy of the university's honor code.

3. What they need (is, are) step-by-step procedures.

4. Either the original or a photocopy (is, are) acceptable as proof.

5. Neither my paralegal nor my assistant (recalls, recall) receiving a letter about that case.

6. Neither the union leader nor the negotiators (has, have) clearly explained their concerns.

7. Neither you nor she (is, are, am) aware of all the implications of the court's decision.

8. The model shown in the recent catalog and advertisements (is, are) not the model I want to buy.

9. The members of the committee (has, have) met to discuss the morale problem.

10. The committee (has, have) met to discuss the morale problem.

11. One of the printers (is, are) being replaced.

12. Our memo, as well as the report issued by the two companies, (was, were) offered as evidence in the trial.

13. Neither of my coworkers (has, have) received a bonus.

14. All of the candidates (is, are) qualified.

15. All of the material (is, are) available at our web site.

16. The analyses of our research group (has, have) rarely been inaccurate.

17. The audience (was, were) thrilled by the magician's performance.

18. The staff (has, have) customarily received their paychecks on Friday.

19. One-half of the documents (has, have) been translated into French.

20. One-half of the document (has, have) been translated into French.

21. Enclosed (is, are) copies of the statements that you requested.

22. The acoustics in the theater in the round (was, were) fantastic.

23. Tim is the specialist who (analyzes, analyze) the information from the bureau.

24. Tim is one of the specialists who (analyzes, analyze) the information from the bureau.

25. Tim is the only one of the specialists who (analyzes, analyze) the information from the bureau.

# Confidence Check Answers

1. Both <u>José</u> and <u>Martha</u> *are* on vacation this week. (The compound subject *José and Martha* requires the plural verb *are*.)

2. <u>Every</u> <u>student</u> and <u>parent</u> *has* received a copy of the university's honor code. (Because the compound subject *student and parent* is preceded by the word *every*, the verb must be singular.)

3. <u>What they need</u> *are* step-by-step <u>procedures</u>. (The clause *What they need* is the subject of the sentence. The plural noun *procedures* determines the verb *are*.)

4. Either the <u>original</u> or a <u>photocopy</u> *is* acceptable as proof. (Because the two subjects are joined by *either...or,* the verb must agree with the subject closer to the verb. The singular word *photocopy* is closer to the verb; therefore, the verb *is* is singular.)

5. Neither my <u>paralegal</u> nor my <u>assistant</u> *recalls* receiving a letter about that case. (Because the two subjects are joined by n*either...nor,* the verb must agree with the subject closer to the verb. The singular word *assistant* is closer to the verb; therefore, the verb *recalls* is singular.)

6. Neither the union <u>leader</u> nor the <u>negotiators</u> *have* clearly explained their concerns. (Because the two subjects are joined by n*either...nor,* the verb must agree with the subject closer to the verb. The plural word *negotiators* is closer to the verb; therefore, the verb *have* is plural.)

7. Neither <u>you</u> nor <u>she</u> *is* aware of all the implications of the court's decision. (Because the two subjects are joined by n*either...nor,* the verb must agree with the subject closer to the verb. The singular word *she* is closer to the verb; therefore, the verb *is* is singular.)

8. The <u>model</u> shown in the recent catalog and advertisements *is* not the model I want to buy. (The word *model* is the singular subject of the sentence; therefore, the verb *is* must be singular. Do not let the intervening words confuse you. Always be sure to locate the main subject before you choose your verb.)

9. The <u>members</u> of the committee *have* met to discuss the morale problem. (The plural subject *members* requires the plural verb *have*.)

10. The <u>committee</u> *has* met to discuss the morale problem. (The singular subject *committee* requires the singular verb *has*.)

11. <u>One</u> of the printers *is* being replaced. (The singular pronoun *one* as the subject of the sentence requires the singular verb *is*.)

12. Our <u>memo</u>, as well as the report issued by the two companies, *was* offered as evidence in the trial. (The singular noun *memo* requires the singular verb *was*. Remember, *and* is the only connective between subjects that will make two singular nouns plural.)

13. <u>Neither</u> of my coworkers *has* received a bonus. (*Neither* is a singular pronoun and, therefore, requires the singular verb *has*.)

14. <u>All</u> of the candidates *are* qualified. (The pronoun *all* is plural in this sentence because it refers to the plural noun *candidates*; therefore, the plural verb *are* is required.)

15. <u>All</u> of the material *is* available at our web site. (The pronoun *all* is singular in this sentence because it refers to the singular noun *material*; therefore, the singular verb *is* is required.)

16. The <u>analyses</u> of our research group *have* rarely been inaccurate. (The plural subject *analyses* requires the plural verb *have*. The singular is *analysis*. Be careful of foreign plurals.)

17. The <u>audience</u> *was* thrilled by the magician's performance. (The collective noun *audience* is functioning as one unit. Therefore, the verb must be singular.)

18. The <u>staff</u> *have* customarily received their paychecks on Friday. (The members of the staff are functioning individually, not as one group. Would you want to share your paycheck with anyone? Therefore, the verb must be plural. If you think the reader will be put off with this grammatical construction, recast the sentence to read as follows: The members of the staff have....)

19. <u>One-half</u> of the documents *have* been translated into French. (The fraction *one-half* refers to the plural noun *documents*; therefore, the plural verb *have* is required.)

20. <u>One-half</u> of the document *has* been translated into French. (The fraction *one-half* refers to the singular noun *document*; therefore, the singular verb *has* is required.)

21. Enclosed *are* <u>copies</u> of the statements that you requested. (The plural subject *copies* follows the verb; therefore, the plural verb *are* is required.)

22. The <u>acoustics</u> in the theater in the round *were* fantastic. (Trust your ear on this one! You would never say, "The acoustics was fantastic.) The noun *acoustics* is plural in this sentence; therefore, the plural *were* is required.)

23. Tim is the specialist <u>who</u> *analyzes* the information from the bureau. (The subject of the dependent clause is the pronoun *who*. The pronoun *who* refers to the noun *specialist*. The noun *specialist* is singular; therefore, the verb *analyzes* must be singular.)

24. Tim is one of the specialists <u>who</u> *analyze* the information from the bureau. (The subject of the dependent clause is the pronoun *who*. The pronoun *who* refers to the noun *specialists*. The noun *specialists* is plural; therefore, the verb *analyze* must be plural. Mentally rearrange the sentence as follows: Of the specialists who analyze....)

25. Tim is the only one of the specialists <u>who</u> *analyzes* the information from the bureau. (The subject of the dependent clause is the pronoun *who*. Because of the words *the only* inserted in the sentence, the pronoun *who* refers to the pronoun *one*. The pronoun *one* is singular; therefore, the verb *analyzes* must be singular.)

## Notes

# Module 6: Pronoun–Antecedent Agreement

## Pronoun–Antecedent Agreement

The concepts of pronoun–antecedent agreement echo the concepts just discussed in the previous module on subject–verb agreement. An antecedent (also known as a *referent*) is the word the pronoun refers to. A pronoun must agree in number (singular or plural), person (first, second, or third), and, if necessary, gender (feminine or masculine) with its antecedent. In the second sentence below, what pronoun would you write on the blank?

❐ Samantha went to the store. _____ bought eggs.

We would all agree that the pronoun *she* belongs in the blank because of the antecedent *Samantha*. The pronoun *she* agrees with the antecedent *Samantha* in number (they are both singular), in person (they are both in the third person), and in gender (they are both feminine).

When the antecedents of a pronoun are joined by *either/or* or *neither/nor*, the pronoun should agree with the nearer antecedent.

❐ Neither the Gagnons nor the Screens have brought **their** binoculars.

❐ Neither the supervisor nor his assistants have reached **their** goals.

❐ Neither the assistants nor the supervisor has reached **his** goals. (Although this sentence is grammatically correct, it is awkward and should be recast. When a plural and a singular are joined with *either/or* or *neither/nor*, the language flows better when the plural antecedent is placed closer to the pronoun.)

❐ Either Rebecca or Juanita will relinquish **her** desk.

❐ Either Robert or Juanita will relinquish **her** desk. (Although this sentence is grammatically correct, it is awkward and should be recast: Robert's or Juanita's desk will have to be relinquished.)

Use a singular pronoun when the antecedent is a singular indefinite pronoun. The following indefinite pronouns are always singular.

| | | | |
|---|---|---|---|
| anyone | everyone | someone | no one |
| anybody | everybody | somebody | nobody |
| anything | everything | something | nothing |
| each | every | either | one |
| each one | many a | neither | another |

❏ Neither one of the campaigns did as well as **it** was supposed to. (The antecedent is *one*, not *campaigns*.)

❏ Every company has **its** own vacation policy.

❏ Everyone should bring **his or her** book to class.

Avoid gender-linked pronouns in genderless situations. When possible, make the antecedent plural to avoid excessive use of *he or she* or *he/she* constructions.

❏ A nurse offers tender loving care to **his or her** patient.

❏ Nurses offer tender loving care to **their** patients.

❏ Somebody left **his or her** wallet in the conference room.

❏ Somebody left **a** wallet in the conference room.

❏ Each defendant has the right to **his or her** day in court.

❏ Defendants have the right to **their** day in court.

Collective nouns, such as *association* and *group,* usually take singular verbs and singular pronouns. Be consistent. Once you establish a collective as singular, keep it singular throughout the sentence.

❏ Our staff will have **its** monthly meeting on Friday.

❏ The committee has submitted **its** final report.

Because indefinite pronouns express the third person, pronouns referring to these antecedents should also be in the third person (*he, she, it, they, him, her, them).*

❏ If anyone wants to attend a training program, **he or she** should apply in writing.

❏ If **you** want to attend a training program, **you** should apply for it in writing.

NOT

❏ If anyone wants to attend a training program, **you** should apply in writing.

The second person pronoun *you* cannot be used in the dependent clause.

Because *anyone* is an indefinite pronoun, it is in the third person; the pronoun *you* is in the second person. They do not agree.

Usually, it is advisable to write out the problem by using the pronoun *who*.

❏ Anyone **who** wants to attend a training program should apply in writing.

The plural pronoun *those* can also be used.

❏ **Those** who want to attend a training program should apply for it in writing.

# Confidence Check

In the following sentences, decide if each pronoun agrees with its antecedent. If the pronoun usage is correct, write "Correct." If the usage is incorrect, correct the error.

1. When these procedures are completed, it will substantiate our claim.

2. Has anyone turned in their vacation request?

3. If an actor is typecast, a director is likely to never offer them a different role.

4. When one has made a promise, it is important that you not renege.

5. Each person must decide the best way to fulfill their career ambitions.

6. Either the van or the truck has their annual overhauling this month.

7. The family are going on their vacation in July.

8. A person needs someone to turn to when they are lonely.

9. The jury has delivered their verdict.

10. The Blue Team has already passed their quota.

11. The staff will start work on their new project tomorrow.

12. The subcommittee has not yet released its findings.

13. Channel 5 is proud of their programming for the next season.

14. If someone has developed a sensitivity to certain antibiotics, you will need to tell your pharmacist.

15. Everyone has completed his course evaluation form.

16. A researcher specializing in DNA may discover they have found only the tip of the iceberg.

17. Someone has left his keys at the checkout counter.

18. Unanimously, the faculty expressed their dissatisfaction with the new policy to increase class size.

19. Neither the coach nor the manager has submitted their resignation.

20. Neither the candidates nor the debate moderator did their best to answer the voter's question.

# Possible Confidence Check Answers

1. When these procedures are completed, *they* will substantiate our claim. (The plural pronoun *they* is needed to agree with the plural antecedent *procedures*.)

2. Has anyone turned in *his/her* vacation request? (The singular pronoun *his/her* is needed to agree with the singular antecedent *anyone*. Or the sentence could be recast as follows: Have any *employees* turned in *their* vacation requests?)

3. If an actor is typecast, a director is likely to never offer *him/her* a different role. (The singular pronoun *him/her* is needed to agree with the singular antecedent *actor*. Or the sentence could be recast in the plural: If *actors* are typecast, a director is likely to never offer *them* a different role.)

4. When you have made a promise, it is important that you not renege. (Since the pronoun *one* is in the third person and the pronoun *you* is in the second person, the sentence needs to be recast: When one has made a promise, it is important not to renege.)

5. Each person must decide the best way to fulfill *his/her* career ambitions. (The singular pronoun *him/her* is needed to agree with the singular antecedent *person*. Or the sentence could be recast by deleting the pronoun: Each person must decide the best way to fulfill career ambitions.)

6. Either the van or the truck has *its* annual overhauling this month. (The singular pronoun *its* is needed to agree with the singular antecedent *truck*.)

7. The family are going on their vacation in July. (This sentence is correct. The plural verb *are* indicates that the members of the family are taking separate vacations. The sentence may flow better as follows: The family members are going on their vacations in July. If the family is taking one vacation together, the sentence could be written as follows: The family is going on *its* vacation in July. Another alternative would be to delete the pronoun *its*.)

8. A person needs someone to turn to when lonely. (The best way to correct this sentence is to delete the pronoun.)

9. The jury has delivered *its* verdict to the judge. (The jury is working together as one collective unit; therefore, the singular pronoun *its* is required.)

10. The Blue Team has already passed *its* quota. (The Blue Team is working together as one collective unit; therefore, the singular pronoun *its* is required.)

11. The staff will start work on *its* new project tomorrow. (The staff is working together as one collective unit; therefore, the singular pronoun *its* is required. If the staff members were working on individual projects, *project* would have to be plural.)

12. The subcommittee has not yet released *its* findings. (This sentence is correct. The singular pronoun *its* refers to the singular noun *subcommittee*.)

13. Channel 5 is proud of *its* programming for the next season. (Channel 5 is a collective noun; therefore, the singular pronoun *its* is required.)

14. Someone *who* has developed a sensitivity to certain antibiotics will need to tell *the* pharmacist. (The best solution is to use the pronoun *who* to refer to the indefinite pronoun *someone* and use the article *the* instead of a possessive pronoun.)

15. Everyone has completed *the* course evaluation form. (The best solution is to use the article *the* instead of a possessive pronoun.)

16. A researcher specializing in DNA may discover *he/she has* found only the tip of the iceberg. (The singular pronoun *his/her* is needed to agree with the singular antecedent *researcher*. Or the sentence could be recast in the plural: Researchers specializing in DNA may discover they have hit only the tip of the iceberg.)

17. Someone has left keys at the checkout counter. (The best solution is to delete the pronoun.)

18. Unanimously, the faculty expressed *its* dissatisfaction with the new policy to increase class size. (The word *unanimously* indicates that the faculty is working together as one unit; therefore, the singular pronoun *its* is required.)

19. Neither the coach nor the manager has resigned. (To avoid using the singular pronoun *his* for agreement, which is awkward, replace the phrase *submitted their resignation* with *resigned*.)

20. Neither the candidates nor the debate moderator tried to answer the voter's question. (This sentence would be awkward if the correct pronoun *his* were to replace the plural pronoun *their* and should, therefore, be recast.)

# Module 7: Pronoun Case

Pronouns are often a problem for writers and editors. However, they need not be. Most of the time—I repeat—*most of the time*, trust your ear. Although sound is not a rule, most of us use pronouns correctly. There are a few trouble spots where your ear may lead you astray. Often, what the ear will accept in the spoken language, the eye will dissect in the written language. Having a few tricks up your sleeve may solve your problems.

Pronouns, words that replace nouns, have three forms (cases) that reflect the role the pronoun plays in the sentence. Pronouns can function as subjects (nominative or subjective case), as objects (objective case), and as indications of possession or ownership (possessive case).

| | Nominative<br><br>____ gave Eric a book. | Objective<br><br>Eric gave a book to ____. | Possessive<br><br>Here is ____ book.<br><br>*This book is ____.* |
|---|---|---|---|
| **First Person** | I, we | me, us | my, our |
| | | | mine, ours |
| **Second Person** | you, you | you, you | your |
| | | | yours |
| **Third Person** | he, she, it, they | him, her, it, them | his, her, their |
| | | | his, hers, theirs |
| **Relative Pronouns** | who | whom | whose |
| | | | whose |

# Nominative and Objective Case

## Nominative Case

Use the nominative case when the pronoun is the subject of the verb. When you have a compound subject, look at each part separately.

- ❑ **She** will purchase the scanner tomorrow.

- ❑ **She** and **he** will purchase the scanner tomorrow.

Use the nominative case after a form of the verb *to be*. A noun or pronoun that follows a form of the verb *to be* is called the predicate nominative. Although this pronoun choice may not always be used in the spoken language, it is the correct form for formal written English. Commonly used forms of *to be* include *am, are, is, was, were, will be, has been.* To test if you have selected the correct form, flip the position of the pronoun and the subject of *to be.* If the pronoun functions in the subject slot, you have selected the nominative case. Here is a trick that may help you.

We would all agree with the following: 2 + 2 = 4. We would also agree that we can turn this math sentence around, and it will still be true: 4 = 2 + 2. Think of each form of *to be* (*am, are, is, was, were, will be, has been, will have been,* etc.) as an equal sign. Let's see how this works.

If we say the following: **She is the millionaire**.

Then we can turn the sentence around and say the following: **The millionaire is she**.

Let's try a couple more:

- ❑ **They** are the millionaires.

- ❑ The millionaires are **they**.

- ❑ **He** and **she** are the millionaires.

- ❑ The millionaires are **he** and **she**. (Whenever you have a compound, do one part at a time.)

So? Is the following right or wrong? **Toys 'R Us**.

Turn the sentence around: **Us 'R Toys**.

The store should be renamed **Toys 'R We**.

## Objective Case

Use the objective case when the pronoun is the object of a verb, a verbal, or a preposition. Trust your ear on these constructions. When you have a compound object, look at each part separately.

- ❐ George remembered **him**.

- ❐ The supervisor spoke to her staff, addressing **them** directly and forthrightly.

- ❐ Susan ordered the scanner for **me** and **her**.

## Confidence Check

Choose the correct form in parentheses.

1. Either Meryl or (I, me) will handle this case.

2. It could have been (he, him) who took the call.

3. Was it Nicholas or (she, her) who spoke at the conference?

4. They promoted Louise and (I, me) to managerial positions.

5. The information was intended for Ethan and (she, her).

# Confidence Check Answers

1. I (The pronoun *I* is the subject of the verb; therefore, the nominative case is needed. I will handle this case.)

2. he (The pronoun is following a form of *to be*; therefore, the independent clause can be turned around: He could have been it.)

3. she (The pronoun is following a form of *to be*; therefore, the independent clause can be turned around: She was it. Be sure to take apart the compound.)

4. me (Do each part of the compound separately. They promoted me.)

5. her (Do each part of the compound separately. The information was intended for her.)

# Possessive Case

Use the possessive case when the pronoun shows ownership or possession. The possessive case has two forms: one form is used when the pronoun modifies a noun (in this case, the possessive pronoun is functioning as an adjective); the other form is used when the pronoun stands alone.

❑ I placed **my** book on **your** desk.

❑ This book is **mine;** that book is **yours.**

In a comparison, the nominative or the objective case could be correct after the words *than* or *as*. Mentally complete the comparison to determine the correct pronoun case.

❑ I am taller than **he.** (than he is tall)

❑ This proposal will affect us as much as **them.** (as much as it will affect them)

These next two examples are both correct, but each has a different meaning.

❑ Mike likes Monday-night football more than I. (Mike likes Monday-night football more than I like Monday-night football. The comparison is about how each of us likes Monday-night football.)

❑ Mike likes Monday-night football more than me. (Mike likes Monday-night football more than he likes me. The comparison is between how much Mike likes football and how much he likes me. With this sentence, Mike might find himself in divorce court!)

When a noun immediately follows a pronoun, drop the noun. Trust your ear, and use the rules you know to select the correct pronoun case.

❑ **We** editors need a vacation. (We need a vacation.)

❑ They gave **us** editors a much-needed vacation. (They gave us a much-needed vacation.)

When a noun and pronoun are in a compound, drop the noun and use the rules you know to select the correct pronoun case.

❑ My friend and **I** won a free picnic lunch. (I won a free picnic lunch.)

❑ The radio station awarded the free picnic lunch to my friend and **me.** (The radio station awarded the free picnic lunch to me.)

Use the possessive case in front of a gerund. A gerund is an *-ing* form of a verb that is functioning like a noun. Remember, adjectives modify nouns; therefore, a gerund should be modified by the possessive case. The following words are examples of possible gerunds: *running, skiing, thinking, conforming, removing.* Sometimes you can change the gerund to another form of the noun. Look at the following examples.

❑ They approved of **our** enrolling in this night class. (They didn't approve of us; they approved of the enrollment.)

❑ I dislike **his** behaving like a fool. (I don't dislike him. He's my son. I love him. I dislike the behavior.)

# Confidence Check

Choose the correct form in parentheses.

1. That manual is (hers, her's).

2. The professor expects (we, us) research students to keep accurate logs.

3. I understood (their, them) declining our offer.

4. We appreciate (you, your) reviewing the proposal.

5. The joke offended Gavin more than (she, her).

6. The director is as concerned as (we, us).

# Confidence Check Answers

1. hers (The word *her's* does not exist in the language.)

2. us (Drop the noun and then select the correct pronoun. The professor expects us to keep accurate logs.)

3. their (The possessive *their* is needed to modify the gerund *declining*. We don't understand everything about them, just their decision to decline the offer.)

4. your (The possessive *your* is needed to modify the gerund *reviewing*. We don't appreciate you; we don't even like you. We appreciate the reviewing.)

5. her (Mentally complete the comparison. The joke offended Gavin more than it offended her.)

6. we (Mentally complete the comparison. The director is as concerned as we are.)

# The Pronouns *Who* and *Whom*

People are often confused by the pronouns *who* and *whom*. Determine the use of the relative pronoun *who* or *whom* by how the pronoun functions in the clause it introduces. Use *who* when the pronoun functions as a subject and *whom* when the pronoun functions as an object.

I'll give you a trick, and you will never get the two pronouns mixed up again. But you must do the trick correctly. The easy way to determine how the pronoun is functioning is to use the following *he-him* test:

Identify the dependent clause that *who* or *whom* introduces and drop *who* or *whom*. Work only with the words to the right of the pronoun that you just dropped (this is the most important part of the trick.) When you read the group of words that is left, there will be a gap in thought. Make the word group into a sentence by inserting either *he* or *him*. Do not change the word order, replace words, delete words other than *who* or *whom*, or add any words other than *he* or *him*. If you inserted *he*, select *who*. If you inserted *him*, select *whom*.

Here's an example of how this works:

  ❏ Sam is the one (who, whom) will be hired.

Isolate the clause: *(who, whom) will be hired*.

Drop *who* or *whom*: *will be hired*.

Notice the gap in thought: _____ *will be hired*.

Insert *he* into gap: *He will be hired.*

Make your who/whom choice: *who will be hired*.

Review the correct sentence: **Sam is the one who will be hired.**

Here's one more example:

  ❏ Sam is the one (who, whom) he will hire.

Isolate the clause: *(who, whom) he will hire*.

Drop *who* or *whom*: *he will hire*.

Notice the gap in thought: *he will hire* _____.

Insert *him* into the gap: *He will hire him.*

Make your who/whom choice: *will hire whom*.

Review the correct sentence: **Sam is the one whom he will hire.**

Remember to ignore the rest of the sentence when doing the trick because other words in the original sentence can trip you up and keep you from selecting the correct pronoun.

Another way to check if you are correct is to do a *verb check*. If every verb in each clause already has a subject, you know that the pronoun will have to be in the objective case. In the first example above, *Sam* is the subject of the verb *is* in the independent clause. The verb *will be hired* in the dependent clause has no subject; therefore, the subjective case must be used. In the second example, *Sam* is again the subject of the verb *is* in the independent clause. The verb *will hire* in the dependent clause has *he* as the subject; therefore, the subjective case cannot be used. The correct form has to be in the objective case.

# Confidence Check

Choose the correct form in parentheses.

1.  We will appoint (whomever, whoever) presents the best information.

2.  The accountant (who, whom) I trust has filed an extension for me.

3.  We need a manager (who, whom) understands the details of this project.

4.  Eva is the board official (who, whom) they were praising.

5.  Elaine, (who, whom) I consider to be a great cook, served a fabulous meal.

6.  Give this letter to (whoever, whomever) arrives first.

# Confidence Check Answers

1. whoever (The pronoun *whoever* is the subject of the verb *presents*.)
2. whom (The pronoun *whom* is the object of the verb *trust*.)
3. who (The pronoun *who* is the subject of the verb *understands*.)
4. whom (The pronoun *whom* is the object of the verb *praising*.)
5. whom (The pronoun *whom* is the object of the verb *consider*.)
6. whoever (The pronoun *whoever* is the subject of the verb *arrives*.)

# Confidence Check

If you find an error in pronoun case, correct the error. If the sentence is correct as written, write *Correct*.

1. I gave a copy of the brochure to whomever requested one.

2. This gift is for my relative who I will be visiting next week.

3. I received confirmations from whomever we had notified last week.

4. Our new accountant is not her, as you were led to believe, but Rosa.

5. It is they who should be held accountable for the accident, not the electrician.

6. We three proofreaders are always expected to work the night shift.

7. Cynthia and me will be attending the meeting instead of Mr. Canders.

8. The new procedure should help the Distribution Office as much as we.

9. I approve of you discussing the issue with the other people in your department.

10. The new information is a critical aid to us understanding the issue.

11. This is a question for you and them to decide.

12. I think us educators deserve more respect.

13. I told you the culprit was she.

14. I was shocked at him behaving that way.

15. Be sure that everything is put in it's place.

16. David, Katie, and her listened to the speaker.

17. Nicholas and he idolize Michael Jordan.

18. She is the person who arranged the party.

19. This morning on Burke Lake Road a reckless bicyclist nearly ran into four of us pedestrians.

20. The mechanic wiped the grease from his hands and explained to Roger and I what had to be done.

21. The guilty person could not possibly have been she.

22. Pepper is not a very good watch dog; he is friendly to whomever pets him.

23. No one was more surprised than I to learn of you joining the army.

24. The sound and light systems in the concert hall are appreciated by we regular symphony patrons.

25. Smythe is the only candidate who the experts consider capable of defeating the incumbent.

# Confidence Check Answers

1. I gave a copy of the brochure to *whoever* requested one. (The pronoun is the subject of the verb. He requested one.)

2. This gift is for my relative *whom* I will be visiting next week. (The pronoun is the object of the verb. I will be visiting him next week.)

3. I received confirmations from *whomever* we had notified last week. (Correct. We had notified him last week.)

4. Our new accountant is not *she*, as you were led to believe, but Rosa. (The nominative case follows a form of *to be*. You can turn the sentence around. She is not our new accountant.)

5. It is *they* who should be held accountable for the accident, not the electrician. (Correct. The nominative case follows a form of *to be*. You can turn the sentence around. They are it.)

6. *We* three proofreaders are always expected to work the night shift. (Correct. Drop off the noun and its adjectives. We are always expected to work the night shift.)

7. Cynthia and *I* will be attending the meeting instead of Mr. Canders. (Take the compound apart. The pronoun is the subject of the sentence. I will be attending the meeting instead of Mr. Canders.)

8. The new procedure should help the Distribution Office as much as *us*. (Mentally complete the comparison. The new procedure should help the Distribution Office as much as it should help us.)

9. I approve of *your* discussing the issue with the other people in your department. (A possessive is used to modify a gerund, which is a noun. I don't approve of you. I approve of the discussion.)

10. The new information is a critical aid to *our* understanding the issue. (A possessive is used to modify a gerund, which is a noun. The information is not a critical aid to us. It is a critical aid to the understanding of the issue.)

11. This is a question for you and *them* to decide. (Correct. Take the compound apart. This is a question for them to decide.)

12. I think *we* educators deserve more respect. (Drop the noun following the pronoun. I think we deserve more respect.)

13. I told you the culprit was *she*. (Correct. The nominative case follows a form of *to be*. You can turn the sentence around. She was the culprit.)

14. I was shocked at *his* behaving that way. (A possessive is used to modify a gerund, which is a noun. I am not shocked at him. I am shocked at his behavior.)

15. Be sure that everything is put in *its* place. (The possessive, not the contraction, is needed to modify the noun *place*.)

16. David, Katie, and *she* listened to the speaker. (The nominative case is used for the subject of a sentence. In a compound subject, drop off the other parts. She listened to the speaker.)

17. Nicholas and *he* idolize Michael Jordan. (Correct. The nominative case is used for the subject of a sentence. In a compound subject, drop off the proper noun. He idolizes Michael Jordan.)

18. *She* is the person *who* arranged the party. (Correct. The nominative case is used for the subject of a sentence. *She* is the subject of *is*. *Who* is the subject of *arranged*. He arranged the party.)

19. This morning on Burke Lake Road a reckless bicyclist nearly ran into four of *us* pedestrians. (Correct. When a noun immediately follows a pronoun, drop the noun and trust your ear. This morning on Burke Lake Road a reckless bicyclist nearly ran into four of us.)

20. The mechanic wiped the grease from his hands and explained to Roger and *me* what had to be done. (In a compound subject, drop off the proper noun. The mechanic wiped the grease from his hands and explained to me what had to be done.)

21. The guilty person could not possibly have been *she*. (Correct. The nominative case follows a form of *to be*. You can turn the sentence around. She could not possibly have been the guilty person.)

22. Pepper is not a very good watch dog; *he* is friendly to *whoever* pets him. (*He* is correct as it is the subject; *whoever* is the subject of *pets*.)

23. No one was more surprised than *I* to learn of *your* joining the army. (A possessive is used to modify a gerund, which is a noun. I am not surprised to learn about you. I know you exist. I am surprised at the joining.)

24. The sound and light systems in the concert hall are appreciated by *us* regular symphony patrons. (When a noun follows a pronoun, drop the noun and its modifiers and trust your ear. The sound and light system in the concert hall are appreciated by us.)

25. Smythe is the only candidate *whom* the experts consider capable of defeating the incumbent. (Use the who/whom trick. The experts consider him capable of defeating the incumbent.)

# Notes

# Module 8: Parallelism

## Parallelism

Parallelism is the gimmick that allows us to get away with a longer sentence. The brain says, "I'm out of here," after about twenty words. But often we can keep our reader with us if we make sure that all parts of each sentence are in the same grammatical form. Parallelism means that coordinate or balanced ideas are expressed in the same constructions. Nouns must be parallel with nouns, verbs with verbs, phrases with phrases, clauses with clauses, and so forth. For example, *that was forwarded last week* and *that was delivered by my courier service* are parallel constructions. On the other hand, *that was forwarded last week* and *to have been delivered by my courier service* are not parallel. Lack of parallelism is a very common problem.

Parallel sentences can add coherence to passages that deserve special attention. This rhetorical device is often used in the best speeches.

Use the device of parallel sentences sparingly. If it is overused, your letters and reports will have an overblown quality.

## Maintaining Parallelism

Maintain parallelism in the following instances:

### Items in a Series

A series consists of three or more elements. Although the repetition of the construction is essential, the repetition of the tag word (in, the, of, for, to) is optional. If the parallel elements are long or deserve special emphasis, use the tag word. If not, omit it.

- ❏ She maintained a tight schedule by **working forty hours a week, training for the marathon, studying for chemistry,** and **socializing with her friends.**

- ❏ The restaurant is famous **for its elaborate menu, for its good service,** and **for its exorbitant prices.**

## Coordinate Ideas

Coordinate ideas are connected by coordinating conjunctions such as *for, and, nor, but, or, yet*. Also, maintain parallelism for ideas in comparisons created by *than* or *as*.

- ❑ Political candidates often try **to discredit their opponents** or **to confuse the voters.**

- ❑ She was in the hospital because she liked **singing in the rain** and **dancing in the shower.**

## Ideas in a Vertical List

Don't mix complete sentences, single words, and different types of phrases in the same list.

The order of business will be as follows:

- ❑ **Hear** the reports of the subcommittees

- ❑ **Create** a procedure for updating employees' computers

- ❑ **Revise** the employee handbook

## Items with Two-Part Connectives

Two-part connectives (correlative conjunctions) include *either/or, neither/nor, not only/but also, both/and*. Make sure that the type of construction following the first connective is the same type following the second connective. Helping verbs such as "have" and "can" are especially troublesome. If the helping verb is shared by both main verbs, place the helping verb before the first connective. If the helping verb is not shared, place it after the connective. Notice that all four of the following sentences are parallel.

- ❑ Either **Eric will go to the party with his friends,** or **he will go to the movie with his sister.**

- ❑ Eric either **will go to the party with his friends** or **will go to the movie with his sister.**

- ❑ Eric will either **go to the party with his friends** or **go to the movie with his sister**.

- ❑ Eric will go either **to the party with his friends** or **to the movie with his sister**.

# Confidence Check

Correct the faulty parallelism in the following sentences. (There is more than one way to correct each sentence.)

1. We hired the applicant because she seemed enthusiastic and because of her expertise in the field.

2. After removing everything in the storage cabinets, scrubbing each shelf, and having ripped out the old shelf paper, Nancy realized that she had forgotten to buy new shelf paper.

3. Three reasons that restaurants cannot find good employees are the competitive job market, wages are low, and lack of training.

4. He wanted to either join the Marines, or he wanted to accept a job as supervisor of a local construction company.

5. Our plan is as follows:

   ❏ Call a meeting of all trainers.

   ❏ Brainstorming ideas for new workshops.

   ❏ We should hire more instructors.

   ❏ To update the manuals.

6. They not only bought a new house this year, but also they went on a cruise to Alaska.

7. The organization hired me to interview each staff member, make a compilation of the areas of concern, that I should create a style manual, and conduct seminars in using the new manual.

8. David wanted to both work in the summer and during the school year.

9. To lose weight and stay healthy, you should follow a low-fat diet, be sure to keep a log of what you eat, avoidance of too many calories, exercising thirty minutes daily, and taking vitamins.

10. To organize for the retirement party, we need to do the following:

    ❏ A date

    ❏ Make a guest list

    ❏ Buying invitations

    ❏ Interview of caterers

    ❏ A discussion with a party planner

    ❏ Collection of money for a joint gift

# Possible Confidence Check Answers

1. We hired the applicant because of *her enthusiasm* and *her expertise in the field*. (Two items joined by *and* must be parallel. A clause and a phrase are not parallel. Changing the clause *she seemed enthusiastic* to the phrase *because of her enthusiasm* makes the sentence parallel. The preposition *because of* is understood before *her expertise in the field*. You could have made both parts into clauses.)

2. After *removing* everything in the storage cabinets, *scrubbing* each shelf, and *ripping* out the old shelf paper, Nancy realized that she had forgotten to buy new shelf paper. (Items in a series must be parallel. Changing *having ripped* to *ripping* makes the phrases all gerunds.)

3. Three reasons that restaurants cannot find good employees are *the competitive job market*, *low wages*, and *lack of training*. (Items in a series must be parallel. Changing the clause *wages are low* to the phrase low wages makes the items all noun phrases.)

4. Either *he wanted to join the Marines*, or *he wanted to accept a job as supervisor of a local construction company*. (The correlative conjunctions *either...or* are now connecting two independent clauses.)

   He either *wanted to join the Marines* or *wanted to accept a job as supervisor of a local construction company*. (The correlative conjunctions *either...or* are now connecting two verb phrases.)

   He wanted either *to join the Marines* or *to accept a job as supervisor of a local construction company*. (The correlative conjunctions *either...or* are now connecting two infinitive phrases.)

   He wanted to either *join the Marines* or *accept a job as supervisor of a local construction company*. (The correlative conjunctions *either...or* are now connecting two infinitive phrases with the tag word *to*.)

5. Our plan is as follows:

   ❏ *Call* (*Calling*) a meeting of all trainers.

   ❏ *Brainstorm* (*Brainstorming*) ideas for new workshops.

   ❏ *Hire* (*Hiring*) more instructors.

   ❏ *Update* (*Updating*) the manuals. (The list can be made parallel by putting items in the same form. I have shown verb phrases and gerunds. You could have made each item a complete sentence.)

6. They not only *bought a new house this year* but also *went on a cruise to Alaska*. (Each part of the correlative *not only...but also* is now followed by a verb phrase.)

7. The organization hired me to *interview* each staff member, *compile* a list of the areas of concern, *create* a style manual, and *conduct* seminars in using the new manual. (The items in the series are now all verb phrases with *to* as the tag word.)

8. David wanted to work both *in the summer* and *during the school year*. (Each part of the correlative is now followed by a prepositional phrase.)

9. To lose weight and stay healthy, you should follow a low-fat diet, keep a log of what you eat, avoid too many calories, exercise thirty minutes daily, and take vitamins. (The items in the series are now verb phrases.)

10. To organize for the retirement party, we need to do the following:

   ❒ *Determine* a date

   ❒ *Make* a guest list

   ❒ *Buy* invitations

   ❒ *Interview* caterers

   ❒ *Discuss* ideas with a party planner

   ❒ *Collect* money for a joint gift

   Each item in the list now begins with a verb. You could have made each item into a gerund or a complete sentence.

## Notes

# Module 9: Modifiers

## Modifiers

In many languages the placement of a modifier—whether a single word, a phrase, or a clause—does not matter. However, in the English language the placement is very important. Incorrect placement can often lead to an ambiguous or a nonsensical meaning. A modifier should be placed so that the writer's intended meaning is clear. Four problems may potentially occur with the placement of modifiers: squinting modifiers, misplaced modifiers, dangling modifiers, and the careless placement of *only*.

## Squinting Modifiers

Sometimes the modifier is placed so that the meaning is ambiguous. It is not clear whether the modifier belongs with one part of the sentence or with another part. Move the squinting modifier so that the meaning is no longer ambiguous, or use *that* to cluster the modifier appropriately.

- ❐ The marathon coordinator said **Friday** we would have a trial run.—**Squinting** (Did the coordinator give this information on Friday, or is the trial run on Friday?)

- ❐ **Friday** the marathon coordinator said we would have a trial run.—**Clear**

- ❐ The marathon coordinator said we would have a trial run on **Friday**.—**Clear**

- ❐ The marathon coordinator said that **Friday** we would have a trial run.—**Clear**

- ❐ The marathon coordinator said **Friday** that we would have a trial run.—**Clear**

- ❐ The company representative told us **eventually** the president would meet with us.—**Squinting** (Did the representative eventually tell us, or would the president eventually meet with us?)

- ❐ The company representative **eventually** told us the president would meet with us.—**Clear**

- ❐ The company representative told us the president would **eventually** meet with us.—**Clear**

# Misplaced Modifiers

Sometimes if the modifier is misplaced, the meaning is entirely different from what the writer intended. Move the modifier or rewrite the entire sentence.

- ❐ The campers spotted the remains of a rattlesnake **walking along the trail. —Misplaced** (Was a dead snake walking along the trail?)

- ❐ **Walking along the trail,** the campers spotted the remains of a rattlesnake.—**Clear**

- ❐ For the holidays I decorated my home **with various relatives and neighbors.—Misplaced** (Were the relatives and neighbors being hung around the house?)

- ❐ **Together with various relatives and neighbors,** I decorated my home.—**Clear**

# Dangling Modifiers

When a sentence begins with a verbal phrase, the phrase modifies the first noun or pronoun that immediately follows the comma. A verbal phrase can have a present participle (*walking*), a past participle (*walked*), or an infinitive (*to walk*). If the verbal phrase does not logically modify the closest noun or pronoun, this incorrect construction is called a dangling modifier.

- ❐ **Walking to school,** the children saw an accident.—**Clear**

- ❐ **Lurking in the shadows,** the tall, dark, scary, disgusting, filthy, gross, pock-marked woman scared me.—**Clear** (Notice that although seven adjectives precede the noun, the sentence is clear because the verbal phrase clearly modifies the first noun [woman] that follows the phrase.)

- ❐ **Running to the train,** Eric's glasses broke.—**Dangling Modifier.** (Were Eric's glasses running to the train?)

- ❐ **Running to the train,** Eric broke his glasses.—**Clear**

- ❐ **While Eric was running to the train,** he broke his glasses.—**Clear**

- ❐ **While Eric was running to the train,** his glasses broke. —**Clear**

- ❐ **After bandaging the dog,** the cat was fed.—**Dangling Modifier.** (Did the cat bandage the dog?)

- ❐ **After bandaging the dog,** the vet fed the cat.—**Clear**

- ❐ **After the vet bandaged the dog, she fed the cat. —Clear**

- ❐ **After the dog was bandaged,** the cat was fed.—**Clear** (Maybe the vet did not feed the cat; someone else did, but we do not know who fed it.)

There are three basic ways to repair misplaced or dangling modifiers:

**Change the phrase to a dependent clause.** Dependent clauses cannot dangle because they contain their own subject and verb. This alternative usually works.

**Move the phrase next to the noun or pronoun that is performing the action.** This alternative works only when the performer appears elsewhere in the sentence.

**Move the noun or pronoun that the phrase modifies to the spot after the introductory phrase.** This alternative works only when the noun or pronoun can be supplied.

# Careless Placement of *Only*

The word *only* is often misplaced. It sounds natural almost anywhere in the sentence, but for the meaning of the sentence to be clear, *only* should be placed as close as possible to what it modifies. The word *only* can be used as an adverb or as an adjective and usually precedes the word it is modifying. Some other words that are often misplaced are *almost*, *just*, and *merely*.

❏ I **only** have $5.—**Careless**

❏ I have **only** $5.—**Clear**

❏ I **only** am testing the chemical.—**Careless**

❏ **Only** I am testing the chemical.—**Clear**

❏ I am **only** testing the chemical.—**Clear**

# Confidence Check

In each of the following pairs of sentences, circle the letter of the one that is clearer.

1.
   a. Yesterday on a trip to the shore we counted twelve geese.
   b. Yesterday I counted twelve geese on a trip to the shore.

2.
   a. Remember, you only have three more days before this sale ends.
   b. Remember, you have only three more days before this sale ends.

3.
   a. Patients who take this medication may occasionally notice a few side effects.
   b. Patients who take this medication occasionally may notice a few side effects.

4.
   a. Upon reaching an altitude of 8,000 feet, breathing became difficult.
   b. Upon reaching an altitude of 8,000 feet, we had difficulty breathing.

5.
   a. Having been flattened to a thickness of approximately one-eighth of an inch, the steak is now ready to be grilled.
   b. Having been flattened to a thickness of approximately one-eighth of an inch, you are now ready to grill the steak.

6.
   a. When used as a thickening agent in a soup, most people don't realize that they are eating tapioca.
   b. When tapioca is used as a thickening agent in a soup, most people don't realize that they are eating it.

7.
   a. If you are using our new international credit card when traveling, these problems will not come up.
   b. Using our new international credit card, these problems will not come up when traveling.

8.
   a. Obviously embarrassed by her foolish answer, Julie blushed.
   b. Obviously embarrassed by her foolish answer, Julie's face turned red.

9.
   a. Running into a long-forgotten classmate from Jefferson High School, I could not remember her name.
   b. Running into a long-forgotten classmate from Jefferson High School, her name escaped me completely.

10.
   a. While still in grade school, Grandmother taught me how to knit.
   b. While I was still in grade school, Grandmother taught me how to knit.

# Confidence Check Answers

1.

   a. Yesterday on a trip to the shore we counted twelve geese. (Correct: The phrase *on a trip to the shore* correctly modifies the pronoun *we*.)

   b. Yesterday I counted twelve geese on a trip to the shore. (Misplaced modifier: Were the geese on a short trip?)

2.

   a. Remember, you only have three more days before this sale ends. (Misplaced modifier: *Only* is illogically modifying *have*.)

   b. Remember, you have only three more days before this sale ends. (Correct: The adverb *only* correctly modifies the adjective *three*.)

3.

   a. Patients who take this medication may occasionally notice a few side effects. (Correct: The adverb *occasionally* correctly modifies the verb *notice*.)

   b. Patients who take this medication occasionally may notice a few side effects. (Squinting modifier: Does the adverb *occasionally* modify *take* or *notice*?)

4.

   a. Upon reaching an altitude of 8,000 feet, breathing became difficult. (Dangling modifier: Did the breathing reach this altitude?)

   b. Upon reaching an altitude of 8,000 feet, we had difficulty breathing. (Correct: The introductory verbal phrase correctly modifies the pronoun *we*.)

5.

   a. Having been flattened to a thickness of approximately one-eighth of an inch, the steak is now ready to be grilled. (Correct: The introductory verbal phrase correctly modifies *steak*.)

   b. Having been flattened to a thickness of approximately one-eighth of an inch, you are now ready to grill the steak. (Dangling modifier: Were you flattened to a thickness of one-eighth of an inch?)

6.

   a. When used as a thickening agent in a soup, most people don't realize that they are eating tapioca. (Misplaced modifier: Were the people used as a thickening agent?)

   b. When tapioca is used as a thickening agent in a soup, most people don't realize that they are eating it. (Correct: Because the sentence begins with a dependent clause rather than a phrase, the independent clause following the comma is correct.)

7.

   a. If you are using our new international credit card when traveling, these problems will not come up. (Correct: Because the sentence begins with a dependent clause rather than a phrase, the independent clause following the comma is correct.)

   b. Using our new international credit card, these problems will not come up when traveling. (Dangling modifier: Did the problems use the credit card?)

8.
   a. Obviously embarrassed by her foolish answer, Julie blushed. (Correct: The introductory verbal phrase correctly modifies the noun *Julie*.)
   b. Obviously embarrassed by her foolish answer, Julie's face turned red. (Dangling modifier: Was Julie's face embarrassed?)

9.
   a. Running into a long-forgotten classmate from Jefferson High School, I could not remember her name. (Correct: The introductory verbal phrase correctly modifies the pronoun *I*.)
   b. Running into a long-forgotten classmate from Jefferson High School, her name escaped me completely. (Dangling modifier: Did the name run into the classmate?)

10.
   a. While still in grade school, Grandmother taught me how to knit. (Misplaced modifier: Was Grandmother in grade school when she taught her granddaughter to knit?)
   b. While I was still in grade school, Grandmother taught me how to knit. (Correct: Turning the verbal phrase into a clause gives the reader the correct information that I was in grade school, not my grandmother.)

# Confidence Check

Correct the following sentences to eliminate misplaced and dangling modifiers.

1. Traffic was reported to be jammed by the police.

2. The factory reopened after a one-month shutdown on July 1.

3. When packaged in a box, the consumer cannot see the pretzels.

4. Squatting behind the plate, the pitcher was given the signal by the catcher.

5. The plague almost killed half of the population.

6. To be tender and edible, you must marinate the meat for at least four hours.

7. I only am presenting the results of the first study.

8. After saving and scrimping for five years, our dream trip was finally going to happen.

9. After searching through the boxes in the attic, the photograph of my parents' wedding was found.

10. To receive a reply to your inquiry, a self-addressed, stamped envelope must be enclosed.

11. The class I am in now meets twice a week.

12. The whole family complimented Sue on the fine performance she gave as they were leaving the auditorium.

13. We need someone to audit reports with statistical experience.

14. While vacationing, his book was completed.

15. After taking a test, the faculty panel accepted me as a candidate for a degree.

# Possible Confidence Check Answers

1. The police reported the traffic jam. (The original sentence means the police created the traffic jam.)

2. After a one-month shutdown, the factory reopened on July 1. (The original sentence means the factory had a one-month shutdown all in one day.

3. When the pretzels are packaged in a box, the consumer cannot see them. (The original sentence means the consumer was packed in the box.)

4. Squatting behind the plate, the catcher signaled the pitcher. (The original sentence gives new meaning to baseball by having the pitcher squatting behind the plate instead of the catcher.)

5. The plague killed almost half of the population. (The original sentence means that no one died, because the word *almost* is modifying *killed*.)

6. To be tender and edible, the meat must be marinated for at least four hours. (The original sentence means you are tender and edible.)

7. Only I am presenting the results of the first study. (I am the only one making the presentation.)

   or

   I am only presenting the results of the first study. (I am not discussing the results, just presenting them.)

   or

   I am presenting the only results of the first study. (There are no other results.)

   or

   I am presenting the results of only the first study. (I am not presenting the results of the second or third study.)

   or

   I am presenting the results of the first study only. (This has the same meaning as the previous sentence, but has a different emphasis. The original sentence makes no sense.)

8. After saving and scrimping for five years, we could finally go on our dream trip. (The original sentence means that the trip saved and scrimped.)

9. After searching through the boxes in the attic, I found the photograph of my parents' wedding. (The original sentence means that the photograph did the searching.)

10. To receive a reply to your inquiry, you must enclose a self-addressed, stamped envelope. (The original sentence means the envelope wants to receive a reply.)

11. The class I am now in meets twice a week. (I changed my class.)

    or

    The class I am in meets twice a week now. (The meeting times changed. The original sentence makes no sense.)

12. As they were leaving the auditorium, the whole family complimented Sue on her fine performance. (The original sentence means the family was leaving Sue.)

13. We need someone with statistical experience to audit reports. (The original sentence means the reports had statistical experience.)

14. While he was vacationing, his book was completed. (The publisher was printing it.)

    or

    While vacationing, he completed his book. (He finished writing it. The original sentence means the book was on vacation.)

15. After I took a test, the faculty panel accepted me as a candidate for a degree. (The original sentence means the panel took the test for me.)

# Notes

# Supplemental Exercises

## Commas with Restrictive and Nonrestrictive Material

Set off nonrestrictive material with commas. Delete commas that mistakenly set off restrictive material. If the punctuation is correct, write "correct."

1. My best friend as I mentioned earlier will be unable to visit me this year.

2. We agreed however, that we must revise the contract.

3. The cost moreover has become prohibitive.

4. The fairness of the methods, not just the end results, must be closely considered.

5. John Keats the great English poet died when he was only 26.

6. My brother Martin who works in an auto factory was pleased to hear the news.

7. Hiroshima which was destroyed by the world's first atom bomb has never fully recovered from the emotional scars of the destruction.

8. Many of the fountains that were ordered shut down are again flowing.

9. This is the method, which will be most cost-effective.

10. The man, who is wearing the red bow tie, is my uncle.

11. They decided, nevertheless that we lack the staff to undertake this project.

12. Katie Rudolph, the new editorial assistant, just graduated from the University of Virginia.

# Comma Review

Directions: Each of the following sentences has two commas missing. Add the commas where they are necessary and indicate which of the following rules you used.

| | |
|---|---|
| Rule 1. | Before a coordinate conjunction in a compound sentence |
| Rule 2. | In a series |
| Rule 3. | Between coordinate adjectives |
| Rule 4. | After an introductory modifier |
| Rule 5. | To prevent misreading |

1. A tour bus, two taxis and several cars all pulled up at the same time and Ms. Madden had to call for help in directing traffic.

2. Staggering a little under the weight of their packs the girls clambered up the last section of the steep rocky path.

3. The infielder leaped, stretched back to her left and speared the white-hot curving liner for the final out.

4. Before we had run two miles on that hot hilly marathon course two of the leaders had pulled up with leg cramps.

5. One building had water damage several broken windows, and minor structural damage but the rest escaped the tornado unscathed.

6. Instead of returning the girls left immediately with the software, the documentation and several floppy discs.

7. Frightened by the distant mournful howling of the coyote the young campers raced back to camp and into their counselor's tent.

8. I once tried to master a complex puzzling computer program; ever since I've avoided such work like the plague.

9. Although the twins had grown up in separate parts of the country they had similar interests, habits and attitudes.

10. Becca tried to locate the lost file but her efforts were stymied by the careless seemingly random filing system used by the former secretary.

11. Having left the crowd at the picnic the two politicians began the long dull drive to the next campaign rally.

12. Jim had once won a small tinny trophy in a track meet; after that track had always been his favorite sport.

13. After standing the crowd in the enormous brightly decorated auditorium gave the returning heroes a great ovation.

14. Unless they can find a new coach the swim team will try to practice attend meets, and compete without anyone to direct them.

15. We might try to charter a bus to go to the convention or we could ask the older more settled members to drive their cars.

16. The scaffolding, the braces and most of the new brick work collapsed during the storm and the workers had to start all over on that wall.

17. Having found exactly the puppy they wanted to buy the three excited giggling kids ran down the mall to find their parents.

18. The ball hit the edge of the green, paused momentarily and then followed a straight precise line to the center of the cup.

19. After she had worked only a few minutes over the huge pile of coins Julie discovered three old very valuable pennies.

20. My sister has had mumps, measles and chicken pox but her husband has never had any of those childhood diseases.

# Colons and Semicolons

Read each sentence to decide if it is punctuated correctly. If the punctuation is correct, write "correct." If the punctuation is incorrect, correct the error.

1. He brought a thesaurus, a dictionary, a grammar book, and a writing guide, and a style manual and a proofreading workbook were provided by the instructor.

2. The causes of the disease, as discussed by Seigel, Raman, and Brown in their latest article, are found in the environment, but the potential cure for the disease, as detailed by Gavin, Miller, and Ruby, is found in the environment as well.

3. Violence begets violence; nevertheless, films are rated with little regard for this fact.

4. We are concerned about dumping beer cans on Earth, however, no one seems to mind dumping hardware into space.

5. The jobs available are: clerk-typist, secretary, statistician, and chemist.

6. The requisition is for: two typewriters, one word processor, one personal computer, and two computer tables.

7. The Human Resources Department consists of four divisions: Recruitment, Employee Benefits, Training and Development, and the Employee Assistance Program.

8. Complete the following steps to submit your entry: log in to your account, click on entry form, answer the questions, and click *submit*.

9. I write a "Things To Do" list every day, however, I rarely get everything accomplished.

10. The ingredients for the cookies are: flour, brown sugar, regular sugar, butter, eggs, and chocolate chips.

11. The file includes: the original invoice, a revised invoice, a photocopy of the front and back of their check, and a copy of our letter of apology.

12. We need three forms of identification: a birth certificate, a driver's license, and a credit card.

13. This is what you need to do: send a copy of the letter to my office, and keep the original for your records.

14. We traveled to Chicago in one day: then we toured the city.

15. My house is on the west side of town; her house is on the east.

# Minor Marks of Punctuation

Change the incorrect use of parentheses, apostrophes, hyphens, quotation marks, and brackets in the following sentences. If the punctuation is correct, write "correct."

1. The supervisor is out of the office (She is participating in a conference), but Grenda can probably answer your question.

2. You may amortize such costs over 5 years, if you wish. (For more information concerning Government regulations for amortization, see the enclosed brochure.)

3. The proofreader had to do three things: 1) call the copyeditor, 2) compare the tables in the document, and 3) check the font size in the appendix.

4. To simplify your computations, use our chart of interest rates (see page 343.)

5. Mr. Schmidt will leave early for the golf tournament (the tee-off time is 7 a.m.).

6. The manual is her's, not our's.

7. Who's office is this?

8. Mary's and Sue's apartment is near Bethesda.

9. Mary and Sue's apartments are near Bethesda.

10. The childrens' rooms need to be cleaned.

11. Willis' car has a flat tire.

12. Sylvia said that "she would like to trade jobs with me."

13. I enjoyed the article "Discovering the Real Washington".

14. Jeff asked, "Did you get a good fare from the airlines"?

15. Our agency has undergone four RIF's in the past five years.

16. I don't like the way the *i*'s look in this font.

17. The rate of cure has steadily increased since 1995. (See table A).

18. We have three concerns: 1) the economy is weak, 2) interest rates are high, and 3) our target consumption group is aging.

19. We will install custom built shelves in each office.

20. In the 1960's our nation passed historic civil-rights legislation.

21. We need to gauge nation-wide support for our proposal.

22. Our positive name recognition is a result of our greatly-improved product.

23. We need to re-assess our financial plans in light of rising energy costs.

24. He is sure he will be a baseball commentator—nothing else matters to him.

25. All three of our largest departments—Human Resources, Publications, and Research—have undergone recent reorganization.

# Punctuation Review

Correct the punctuation problems in the following sentences. If the punctuation is correct, write "correct."

1. The trends are described in detail in chapter 7 (see pages 76-83).

2. The meeting will take place on May 5 (9 a.m.–3 p.m.)

3. We decided to expand our staff by 70 people, however, the current economic climate has forced us to reconsider.

4. The committee, however, has not decided to hold hearings on the proposed regulation.

5. Susan asked, "Will changes in the system really affect office productivity"?

6. Did Susan ask, "Will changes in the system really affect office productivity"?

7. We toured the new facility, it is perfect for our office.

8. Review the script this evening, we will discuss it at our morning meeting.

9. David has examined our proposal, however, we are awaiting his comments.

10. We wanted to vacation in Sydney; however, finances dictated that we vacation in Bethany Beach instead.

11. Two years ago he promised to speak at this year's convention; but, yesterday he changed his mind.

12. The new driver sat tentatively behind the wheel of his mother's car and his mother sighed deeply as her son turned on the ignition.

13. As the sun set behind the gently rolling hills of Giverny, a rosy glow enveloped the tiny village.

14. Although I enjoy traveling to new places on vacation I am always glad to return home to familiar sights and sounds.

15. I have just finished reading the short story "The Gift of the Magi".

16. My neighbor said, "We need to do something about the deteriorating house across the street."

17. The phrase "sizing up the opponent," often used in political contests, is actually a sports expression.

18. The first-prize poem, "My Homeland", was written by a recent Chinese immigrant.

19. We have completed our fiscal year budget report. (The enclosed executive summary is for your reference).

20. John will be able to purchase a new car, if the car manufacturers implement their proposed rebates.

21. We plan to travel the entire distance to Vermont in one day, unless we get too tired during the trip.

22. The Baltimore Orioles who hope to make the playoffs have acquired a new manager.

23. We plan to move into the new headquarters building which is in downtown Washington.

---

24. The girl who met us at the train station is my sister.

25. Peering at us from behind his wire-rimmed glasses, the desk clerk seemed to be sneering with contempt.

26. To finish the required work by Friday we need to work late every night this week.

27. Taught by teachers without a college diploma the children from the rural district could not compete academically with their suburban counterparts.

28. Erin, a brilliant young lady was recently named one of 100 Presidential Scholars.

29. Fair Oaks Mall, a large shopping complex in Northern Virginia is in the midst of a major refurbishing.

30. We have received requests for information from: IBM, Control Data, Sprint, and IconLogic.

31. Among the reports he has authored are: *Tomorrow's Lakes and Rivers, Our Troubled Environment,* and *Improving Our Air*.

32. The architect has designed the following buildings: the Airey Center in Cleveland, the Fitzpatrick Theater in Boston, and the Museum of the South in Atlanta.

33. He will be attending a 3 day conference in San Diego later this month.

34. We will use only fire tested materials for upholstery in our buildings.

35. Government owned property is exempt from the requirements of the new legislation.

36. Yours is on the table; ours is on the chair.

37. I decided not to purchase the chair because it's fabric is very delicate.

38. The book asks the central question, "Who is responsible for improving the economy in this country...?"

39. On our trip we will visit London, England, June 5-10, Paris, France, June 10-15, Bern, Switzerland, June 15-18, and Munich, Germany, June 18-21.

40. We have considered three different color schemes: mauve, gray, and white, green, rust, and beige, and green, salmon, and off-white.

# Subject–Verb Agreement

Underline the subject of the verb in parentheses and select the correct verb form in each of the following sentences.

1. Both the instructor and the participant (is, are) responsible for creating a positive climate for learning.

2. Every editor and proofreader (has, have) received a copy of the style manual.

3. Neither the donors nor the recipients (has, have) received invitations to the party.

4. Either expenditures or revenue (needs, need) to be adjusted.

5. A group of equations (is, are) included in the appendix.

6. Mickey Manis, as well as several other executives in the workshop, (feels, feel) that this type of seminar is very valuable.

7. Gregory is one of the people who (has, have) been selected to attend the convention.

8. Each of the engineers (has, have) received a copy of the proposal.

9. Some (is, are) still here.

10. All of the books (was, were) returned.

11. The final analyses (is, are) now complete.

12. The criteria for the selection (has, have) been determined.

13. Ten months (is, are) a long time to wait.

14. I just learned that $15,000 (has, have) been donated anonymously.

15. There (is, are) the materials you requested.

16. Here (is, are) a pen and piece of paper.

17. Most of the letter (has, have) been typed.

18. Michael is one of the designers who (has, have) been selected for a special award.

19. Neither of the candidates (has, have) returned from lunch.

20. The committee (has, have) not yet completed its annual report.

21. The manager, along with his assistants, (is, are) attending the meeting.

22. One of the concerns expressed by our assistants (is, are) the need for additional software.

23. The scissors (is, are) on my desk.

24. Fifty percent of the cash (was, were) stolen from the cash register.

25. Fifty percent of the books (was, were) destroyed in the flood.

# Pronoun–Antecedent Agreement

Read each sentence to decide if the pronoun agrees with its antecedent. If the pronoun usage is correct, write "correct." If the usage is incorrect, correct the error.

1. The staff will start work on their new project next week.

2. The committee has not yet released its report.

3. When the jury reaches their verdict, the judge will inform us.

4. If someone has developed a sensitivity to language, you will be very annoyed by grammar errors.

5. Everyone has completed his course workshop assessment.

6. Someone has left his book in the classroom.

7. Everyone has their own definition of "freedom."

8. A doctor should be responsive to the needs of his patients.

9. If the findings are inconclusive, it will not persuade the jury.

10. All employees will begin their vacations next Friday.

11. Neither the players nor the coach has yet made his decision.

12. My friend and adviser offered his suggestions. (Be careful! The same person is the friend and adviser.)

13. The managers and assistant managers must submit their reports by the first of the month.

14. The cast will have their cast party after its final performance.

15. Each of the workers at the concession area should count their money and turn in their receipts at the end of each performance.

16. An usher should put a smile on his face when he seats the patrons.

17. Either the light technician or the prompter will give their key to me.

18. No one can know if they will be promoted this year.

19. An elephant never eats a leaf or bark that has fungus growing on them.

20. Neither of the two computers is known for their reliability.

21. A family should install at least one carbon monoxide detector in their home.

22. Each staff member got a raise on the date of his anniversary with the agency.

23. The human resources department has changed their enrollment process for workshops.

24. When one has received a verbal reprimand from your supervisor, you should take it seriously.

25. The jury has rapidly completed their deliberations.

---

# Pronoun Case

Choose the correct form in parentheses.

### Nominative Pronouns and Objective Pronouns

1. Either Barbara or (I, me) will handle this case.

2. Brian and (I, me) have reviewed the data.

3. It could have been (he, him) who called last night.

4. Was it Jennie or (he, him) who spoke at the conference?

5. The winner was (he, him), not Milton.

6. They promoted Lisa and (I, me) to supervisory positions.

7. The material was intended for Seth and (she, her).

### Possessives, Contractions, and Comparisons

1. That copy is (hers, her's).

2. Juanita is a friend of (ours, our's).

3. I understood (his, him) declining our offer.

4. We appreciate (you, your) reviewing the papers.

5. (You're, Your) assertion is incorrect.

6. (It's, Its) inconceivable that the ruling could be overturned.

7. Eva is brighter than (I, me).

8. The joke offended Ethan more than (she, her).

9. The director is as concerned as (we, us).

### Appositives and Compounds

1. Mr. Porter introduced the award-winning editors, Andy and (I, me).

2. The teacher expects (us, we) students to be perfect.

3. (We, Us) students need to prepare carefully for class.

4. The copies are for George and (I, me, myself).

### Who, Whom, Etc.

1. They will hire (whomever, whoever) is best qualified for the position.

2. The receptionist (who, whom) I upset has filed a grievance against me.

3. We need a manager (who, whom) understands the difficulties of being a working mother in the middle of flu season.

4. Linda is the account representative (who, whom) they were criticizing.

5. Meryl, (who, whom) I consider to be a great homemaker, admits that she hates cooking and cleaning.

6. (Whose, Who's) book is this?

# Pronoun Case Review

Underline the correct form pronoun case.

1.  Marguerite has more education than (I, me), but I am a more conscientious worker.

2.  Please send a brochure to Edward and (I, me).

3.  Julie is as sophisticated as (her, she).

4.  Adam and (I, me) both attended last year's convention.

5.  I suspect that it is (me, I), not Terry, who will be expected to finish the project.

6.  The new representative is (her, she), not James.

7.  I do not object to (you, your) going to the meeting.

8.  I appreciate (him, his) speaking before our group.

9.  I am pleased to introduce the chemist (who, whom) we all admire—Dr. Wang.

10. The economist (who, whom) visited our office may soon become a permanent member of the staff.

11. Clara, Carl, and (her, she) listened to the speaker.

12. Anna helped (they, them) with their work.

13. (His, Him) winning the Academy Award did not surprise the critics.

14. Marilyn and (I, me) attended the luncheon.

15. The Senator arrived with Ms. McCoy and (he, him).

16. He was amazed by (you, your) arriving so early.

17. They thought it was (her, she) who developed the film script.

18. The coach explained the rules to his son and (we, us).

19. That was an exciting proposal presented by Mrs. Phillips and (he, him).

20. Bob and (her, she) derive great pleasure from vacationing at the beach.

21. Some veterinarians are better informed than (her, she).

22. She helped you more than (I, me).

23. A year ago I went to a basketball game with Mitchell and (he, him).

24. Mitchell and (he, him) idolize Michael Jordan.

25. (Him, His) guarding the house helped the old woman.

26. She seems to like Burton more than (I, me).

27. It was (I, me) who voted for you as chairman.

28. The entry form from Mr. Pierce and (her, she) arrived today.

29. She is the person (who, whom) arranged the party.

30. We invited everyone (who, whom) you requested.

# Verb Tense and Mood

Select the correct verb form from the choices given in parentheses.

1. I always thought that Seattle, not Olympia, (is, was) the capital of Washington.

2. I looked at the man warily, (checked, check) his identification, and then called the security desk for help.

3. He was viewed as an authority on the subject because he (studied, had studied) for four years at Harvard University.

4. I (have worked, worked) at this company for 15 years, and I still enjoy my job here.

5. According to the terms of your contract, you (will, shall) submit a weekly progress report.

6. Carla (has drove, has driven) me to work every day this week because my clutch (did not engage, does not engage).

7. I recommend that Debby (is removed, be removed) from the committee.

8. Matthew demanded that Andrew (leaves, leave) the room at once.

9. If I (am, were) your secretary, I would type the report for you. [I am not your secretary.]

10. If I (am, were) appointed chairperson, I will change the meeting format. [I may be appointed chairperson.]

# Verb Forms

Correct the errors in the use of verb forms. If the verb is correct, write "correct."

1. Frank gone to work early every day this week.

2. I have spoke with my supervisor about the vacation schedule.

3. A main water pipe has sprung a leak.

4. I rode the bus to work today.

5. I have never broken a promise to a friend.

# Verb Tense

Correct the verb tense in each of the following sentences. If the verb is correct, write "correct."

1. I was surprised that the study said Washington was not our country's most important city.

2. He walked into the office and starts to complain to me before he even said, "Good morning."

3. I offered Ms. Lewis the job because she already had 10 years of experience in our business.

4. By the time I arrived at the meeting, Kevin already made his presentation.

5. He spoke with the voice of experience because he traveled extensively in Europe from 2009 until this year.

6. The report said that cholesterol was a factor that contributed to heart disease.

7. The teacher told the class, "I enjoyed working with you during the past 10 sessions."

8. I performed at the Arena Stage for the past 10 years.

9. Ginny arrived late to work every morning this week.

10. The police officer told the driver to get out of the car, searched the car for drugs and weapons, and says nothing when he discovers a gun concealed under the front seat.

# Verb Mood

Correct the verb mood in each of the following sentences. If the verb is correct, write "correct."

1. I recommend that she is appointed Director.

2. The President suggested that Chester studies ways to improve the farm aid bill.

3. The Commission urged that Ms. Perez reconsiders submitting her resignation.

4. He insisted that Maria is removed from the room at once.

5. If I was Chairman of the Federal Reserve Board, I would lower interest rates.

6. If I was able to travel for free, I would roam around the world for the rest of my life.

7. If he was more attentive, he would have understood the directions.

8. If she was able to attend, she would have.

9. If my associate arrived at work on time, the report would have been typed by now.

10. If we are able to resolve the problem, morale will improve.

# Verb Tense

Change the verbs in the following paragraph to the appropriate tense to read as if Pepper is no longer living. Your first sentence should read: "Pepper always knew precisely how to annoy someone."

Pepper always knows precisely how to annoy someone. Pepper is a dog, a "regal" blend of Newfoundland and Australian Shepherd, two breeds that guarantee snobbery. This particular dog knows exactly when to come asking for food—just when the other dogs have already been fed and the food has been put away. He understands precisely when to want to go into a room—just when the door has been closed. He is uncanny at knowing exactly where to sit—right where I want to sweep the floor or, more unerringly annoying, right on the dirt I have already swept together. Pepper knows where to sit on a beautiful spring day—on the lounge chair (better known as his "throne") on the deck so no one else can enjoy the lovely weather. He is quite the social butterfly—whenever he hears the neighborhood dogs barking in "dogland," he communicates with them by bellowing his responses. He has the knack for perfect timing—as soon as I snuggle on the sofa with a good book and a steaming cup of tea, he comes behind me and paws the back of the sofa so I will get up and let him out. This dog is certainly the "perfect" dog.

# Parallelism

Correct the faulty parallelism in the following sentences.

1. When touring other countries, he enjoyed eating the native food, visiting museums, and walks through the city.

2. Her new job involves editing newsletter submissions, preparing copy for the printer, and the review of page proofs prepared by the printer.

3. He searched on the top of his cluttered desk, in the overcrowded bookshelves in his office, and he checked through the stacks of papers under his desk.

4. She enjoys reading and the times of snowboarding.

5. He said that there will be promotion opportunities but the limited number of such promotions.

6. Either he must have forgotten our meeting or been caught in traffic.

7. Cynthia neither has the resources to help pay for the party nor the time to help plan it.

8. Please follow this procedure:

    ❒ Reserve the room at least three weeks in advance.

    ❒ You should send us list of the items you will need and a floor plan of the table and chairs.

    ❒ Arriving at least thirty minutes before the workshop begins to verify that the room is arranged as you requested.

# Grammar Review

Correct the grammar problems in the following sentences. If the grammar is correct, write "correct."

1. Either Mrs. Roth or her associates has edited the final draft.
2. Neither Barbara nor Gail have received the material.
3. Mr. Abrams and she will attend the conference in Rome.
4. The company has invited Leah and I to participate in a panel discussion of editorial practices.
5. Neither of the plans have been approved by Mr. Andrews.
6. Either of the alternatives is an appropriate solution to our morale problem.
7. One of the books were left in the auditorium.
8. Each of the invitations is embossed with a gold seal.
9. There are many flights leaving for Boston from Dulles Airport.
10. There is a package and a large envelope for you at the security desk.
11. I insist that he is replaced as chairperson effective this Friday.
12. I move that $200 is appropriated to purchase a scanner.
13. If he was able to speak to the convention, he would do so.
14. If he is able to speak to the convention, he will do so.
15. The phenomena has been observed by many astronomers.
16. The data have been analyzed by our scientists.
17. Anybody who is available to help with registration should contact their local representative.
18. Everybody has a right to express their opinion on the issues.
19. Our new neighbor is as friendly as him.
20. The reorganization has affected Michael more than I.
21. She herself would never attempt such a risky venture.
22. Please send the original pictures and the negatives to Austin and myself.
23. We have sent a brochure to whomever requested one.
24. I would like to introduce Charles Monihan, who we recently selected to serve as office manager.
25. I have discussed the problem with my staff, and they agreed that we must improve our response time to member queries.
26. The PTA lobbies for the educational needs of children, supports teachers in the public schools, and expressed high expectations for the products of American classrooms.
27. The soccer team has won all of their Division 2 games this fall.
28. The group have reached their individual goals for this year.

29. The winner of the annual All-Around Achiever Award is she, not Josh, the expected winner.

30. It is they who will be held accountable for the problems.

31. She is the faster of the two sisters.

32. The defense attorney presented a strong case for his client, but the case presented by the prosecution was the strongest.

33. He moved so quick that he disappeared from the room before I had an opportunity to acknowledge his presence.

34. In public he spoke as smooth as a politician, but in private he was shy and taciturn.

35. I recently learned that English was actually a Germanic language.

36. The report said that potatoes were not fattening.

37. Every manager will receive his copy of the revised manual by Monday.

38. A doctor must strive to meet the needs of his patients.

39. The association will hold their annual convention in Hawaii this winter.

40. The corporation has informed their stockholders that there will be no dividend this quarter.

41. The daily market fluctuations were assessed by the vice president of investments.

42. Fixing the flat tire, the lug wrench broke in the mechanic's hand.

43. Ms. Oliver is the specialist who is assigned to write the proposal.

44. Ms. Oliver is one of the specialists who is assigned to write the proposal.

45. Ms. Oliver is the only one of the specialists who is assigned to write the proposal.

46. The young senator tends to vote conservative.

# Notes

## iCONLOGiC
"Skills and Drills" Learning

# Supplemental Exercises: Answer Key

## Commas with Restrictive and Nonrestrictive Material

1. My best friend, as I mentioned earlier, will be unable to visit me this year. (The clause *as I mentioned earlier* is nonrestrictive and should be set off with commas.)

2. We agreed, however, that we must revise the contract. (The word *however* is nonrestrictive and should be set off with commas.)

3. The cost, moreover, has become prohibitive. (The word *moreover* is nonrestrictive and should be set off with commas.)

4. The fairness of the methods, not just the end results, must be closely considered. (Correct: The phrase *not just the end results* is nonrestrictive and should be set off with commas.)

5. John Keats, the great English poet, died when he was only 26. (The phrase *the great English poet* is nonrestrictive and should be set off with commas.)

6. My brother Martin, who works in an auto factory, was pleased to hear the news. (The clause *who works in an auto factory* is nonrestrictive and should be set off with commas.)

7. Hiroshima, which was destroyed by the world's first atom bomb, has never fully recovered from the emotional scars of the destruction. (The clause *which was destroyed by the world's first atom bomb* is nonrestrictive and should be set off with commas. In addition, the pronoun *which* is used for nonrestrictive clauses.)

8. Many of the fountains that were ordered shut down are again flowing. (Correct: The clause *that were ordered shut down* is restrictive and should not be set off with commas. In addition, the pronoun *that* is used for restrictive clauses.)

9. This is the method that will be most cost-effective. (The clause *that will be most cost-effective* is restrictive and should not be set off with commas. In addition, the pronoun *that* is used for restrictive clauses, so *which* should be changed to *that*.)

10. The man who is wearing the red bow tie is my uncle. (The clause *who is wearing the red bow tie* is restrictive and should not be set off with commas.)

11. They decided, nevertheless, that we lack the staff to undertake this project. (The word *nevertheless* is nonrestrictive and should be set off with commas.)

12. Katie Rudolph, the new editorial assistant, just graduated from the University of Virginia. (Correct: The phrase *the new editorial assistant* is nonrestrictive and should be set off with commas.)

# Comma Review

> Rule 1. Before a coordinate conjunction in a compound sentence
>
> Rule 2. In a series
>
> Rule 3. Between coordinate adjectives
>
> Rule 4. After an introductory modifier
>
> Rule 5. To prevent misreading

*The rule number is in parentheses following the comma.*

1. A tour bus, two taxis,(2) and several cars all pulled up at the same time, (1) and Ms. Madden had to call for help in directing traffic.

2. Staggering a little under the weight of their packs, (4) the girls clambered up the last section of the steep, (3) rocky path.

3. The infielder leaped, stretched back to her left, (2) and speared the white-hot, (3) curving liner for the final out.

4. Before we had run two miles on that hot, (3) hilly marathon course, (4) two of the leaders had pulled up with leg cramps.

5. One building had water damage, (2) several broken windows, and minor structural damage, (1) but the rest escaped the tornado unscathed.

6. Instead of returning, (4 and/or 5) the girls left immediately with the software, the documentation, (2) and several floppy discs.

7. Frightened by the distant, (3) mournful howling of the coyote, (4) the young campers raced back to camp and into their counselor's tent.

8. I once tried to master a complex, (3) puzzling computer program; ever since, (4) I've avoided such work like the plague.

9. Although the twins had grown up in separate parts of the country, (4) they had similar interests, habits and attitudes.

10. Becca tried to locate the lost file, (1) but her efforts were stymied by the careless, (3) seemingly random filing system used by the former secretary.

11. Having left the crowd at the picnic, (4) the two politicians began the long, (3) dull drive to the next campaign rally.

12. Jim had once won a small, (3) tinny trophy in a track meet; after that, (4 and/or 5) track had always been his favorite sport.

13. After standing, (4) the crowd in the enormous, (3) brightly decorated auditorium gave the returning heroes a great ovation.

14. Unless they can find a new coach, (4) the swim team will try to practice, (2) attend meets, and compete without anyone to direct them.

15. We might try to charter a bus to go to the convention, (1) or we could ask the older, (3) more settled members to drive their cars.

16. The scaffolding, the braces, (2) and most of the new brick work collapsed during the storm, (1) and the workers had to start all over on that wall.

17. Having found exactly the puppy they wanted to buy, (4) the three excited, (3) giggling kids ran down the mall to find their parents.

18. The ball hit the edge of the green, paused momentarily, (2) and then followed a straight, (3) precise line to the center of the cup.

19. After she had worked only a few minutes over the huge pile of coins, (4) Julie discovered three old, (3) very valuable pennies.

20. My sister has had mumps, measles, (2) and chicken pox, (1) but her husband has never had any of those childhood diseases.

# Colons and Semicolons

1. He brought a thesaurus, a dictionary, a grammar book, and a writing guide; and a style manual and a proofreading workbook were provided by the instructor. (Usually a comma precedes a coordinating conjunction that joins two independent clauses, but because the clauses have internal commas, a semicolon should precede the coordinating conjunction *and* for clarity for the reader.)

2. The causes of the disease, as discussed by Seigel, Raman, and Brown in their latest article, are found in the environment; but the potential cure for the disease, as detailed by Gavin, Miller, and Ruby, is found in the environment as well. (Usually a comma precedes a coordinating conjunction that joins two independent clauses, but because the clauses have internal commas, a semicolon should precede the coordinating conjunction *but* for clarity for the reader.)

3. Violence begets violence; nevertheless, films are rated with little regard for this fact. (Correct: Because this sentence is composed of two independent clauses joined by the conjunctive adverb *nevertheless*, a semicolon should precede the adverb.)

4. We are concerned about dumping beer cans on Earth; however, no one seems to mind dumping hardware into space. (Because this sentence is composed of two independent clauses joined by the conjunctive adverb *however*, a semicolon should precede the adverb.)

5. The jobs available are clerk-typist, secretary, statistician, and chemist. (No colon should follow the verb *are* because the word group preceding the colon is not a complete sentence.)

6. The requisition is for two typewriters, one word processor, one personal computer, and two computer tables. (No colon should follow the preposition *for* because the word group preceding the colon is not a complete sentence.)

7. The Human Resources Department consists of four divisions: Recruitment, Employee Benefits, Training and Development, and the Employee Assistance Program. (Correct: The colon is used correctly in this sentence. The word group that precedes the colon is a complete sentence. Remember that the word group that follows the colon does not have to be a complete sentence.)

8. Complete the following steps to submit your entry: log in to your account, click on entry form, answer the questions, and click *submit*. (Correct: The colon is used correctly in this sentence. The word group that precedes the colon is a complete sentence.)

9. I write a "Things To Do" list every day; however, I rarely get everything accomplished. (Because this sentence is composed of two independent clauses joined by the conjunctive adverb *however*, a semicolon should precede the adverb.)

10. The ingredients for the cookies are flour, brown sugar, regular sugar, butter, eggs, and chocolate chips. (No colon should follow the verb *are* because the word group preceding the colon is not a complete sentence.)

11. The file includes the original invoice, a revised invoice, a photocopy of the front and back of their check, and a copy of our letter of apology. (No colon should follow the verb *includes* because the word group preceding the colon is not a complete sentence.)

12. We need three forms of identification: a birth certificate, a driver's license, and a credit card. (Correct: The colon is used correctly in this sentence. The word group that precedes the colon is a complete sentence. Remember that the word group that follows the colon does not have to be a complete sentence.)

13. This is what you need to do: send a copy of the letter to my office, and keep the original for your records. (Correct: The colon is used correctly in this sentence. The word group that precedes the colon is a complete sentence. Depending on your style, the *s* in *send* could be capitalized.)

14. We traveled to Chicago in one day; then we toured the city. (Because the second sentence does not explain the previous one, the use of the colon is incorrect. The two independent clauses should be separated by a semicolon because the ideas are closely related. You might say that the second sentence continues the story rather than explains it.)

15. My house is on the west side of town; her house is on the east. (Correct: Because the second sentence does not explain the previous one but rather continues the story, the use of the semicolon is correct.)

# Minor Marks of Punctuation

1. The supervisor is out of the office (she is participating in a conference), but Grenda can probably answer your question. (The first word of a sentence that is embedded in parentheses in another sentence should not be capitalized.)

2. You may amortize such costs over 5 years, if you wish. (For more information concerning Government regulations for amortization, see the enclosed brochure.) (Correct: A complete sentence that stands alone within parentheses should begin with a capital letter and have the terminal punctuation inside the closing parenthesis.)

3. The proofreader had to do three things: (1) call the copyeditor, (2) compare the tables in the document, and (3) check the font size in the appendix. (When numbers are used in a horizontal list, each number should be enclosed in parentheses.)

4. a. To simplify your computations, use our chart of interest rates (see page 343). (The first word of a sentence that is embedded in parentheses in another sentence should not be capitalized, and the terminal punctuation should be placed outside the closing parenthesis.)

   b. To simplify your computations, use our chart of interest rates. (See page 343.) (A complete sentence that stands alone within parentheses should begin with a capital letter, and the terminal punctuation should be placed inside the closing parenthesis.)

5. Mr. Schmidt will leave early for the golf tournament (the tee-off time is 7 a.m.). (Correct: The first word of a sentence that is embedded in parentheses in another sentence should not be capitalized, and the terminal punctuation should be placed outside the closing parenthesis.)

6. The manual is hers, not ours. (Possessive pronouns do not use apostrophes.)

7. Whose office is this? (The possessive pronoun *whose* is needed in this sentence, not the word *who's*, which is a contraction for *who is*.)

8. Mary and Sue's apartment is near Bethesda. (Because Mary and Sue share one apartment, joint possession is necessary. Use an apostrophe only on the noun [owner] closer to the item owned.)

9. Mary's and Sue's apartments are near Bethesda. (Because Mary and Sue have separate apartments, individual possession is necessary. Use an apostrophe on each noun [owner].)

10. The children's rooms need to be cleaned. (Because the plural noun does not end in *s*, an apostrophe and an *s* are added.)

11. Willis' or Willis's car has a flat tire. (Both forms are correct, depending on the rules of the style manual of choice.)

12. Sylvia said that she would like to trade jobs with me. (This is an indirect quote. No quotation marks should be used.)

13. I enjoyed the article "Discovering the Real Washington." (Periods are placed inside closing quotation marks.)

14. Jeff asked, "Did you get a good fare from the airlines?" (A questions mark goes inside closing quotation marks when the quoted words are a question.)

15. Our agency has undergone four RIFs in the past five years. (Usually, plural forms of abbreviations do not use an apostrophe. Be sure to check your style manual.)

16. I don't like the way the *i*'s look in this font. (Correct: The apostrophe is correct for clarity.)

17. a. The rate of cure has steadily increased since 1995. (See table A.) (A complete sentence that stands alone within parentheses should begin with a capital letter, and the terminal punctuation should be placed inside the closing parenthesis.)

    b. The rate of cure has steadily increased since 1995 (see table A). (The first word of a sentence that is embedded in parentheses in another sentence should not be capitalized, and the terminal punctuation should be placed outside the closing parenthesis.)

18. We have three concerns: (1) the economy is weak, (2) interest rates are high, and (3) our target consumption group is aging. (When numbers are used in a horizontal list, each number should be enclosed in parentheses.)

19. We will install custom-built shelves in each office. (A hyphen is used between two words that function as one adjective, known as a unit modifier.)

20. In the 1960s our nation passed historic civil rights legislation. (Usually, plural forms of decades do not use an apostrophe. Be sure to check your style manual.)

21. We need to gauge nationwide support for our proposal. (Words ending with the suffix *-wide* are usually one word. Be sure to check your dictionary and your style manual.)

22. Our positive name recognition is a result of our greatly improved product. (Adverbs ending in *-ly* are never hyphenated.)

23. We need to reassess our financial plans in light of rising energy costs. (Words beginning with the prefix *re-* are usually one word. Be sure to check your dictionary and your style manual.)

24. He is sure he will be a baseball commentator—nothing else matters to him. (Correct: The em dash after the complete sentence is used to emphasize the next sentence.)

25. All three of our largest departments—Human Resources, Publications, and Research—have undergone recent reorganization. (Correct: The em dash that interrupts the complete sentence is used for emphasis and for clarity because of the commas in the series.)

# Punctuation Review

1. a. The trends are described in detail in chapter 7 (see pages 76-83). (Correct: The first word of a sentence that is embedded in parentheses in another sentence should not be capitalized, and the terminal punctuation should be placed outside the closing parenthesis.)

   b. The trends are described in detail in chapter 7. (See pages 76-83.) (Alternate punctuation: A complete sentence that stands alone within parentheses should begin with a capital letter, and the terminal punctuation should be placed inside the closing parenthesis.)

2. The meeting will take place on May 5 (9 a.m.–3 p.m.). (The information in the parentheses is not a complete sentence, so a period needs to be placed outside the closing parenthesis for the terminal punctuation for the sentence.)

3. We decided to expand our staff by 70 people; however, the current economic climate has forced us to reconsider. (Because this sentence is composed of two independent clauses joined by the conjunctive adverb *however*, a semicolon should precede the adverb.)

4. The committee, however, has not decided to hold hearings on the proposed regulation. (Correct: The word *however* is nonrestrictive and should be set off with commas.)

5. Susan asked, "Will changes in the system really affect office productivity?" (A question mark goes inside closing quotation marks when the quoted words are a question.)

6. Did Susan ask, "Will changes in the system really affect office productivity?" (A question mark goes inside closing quotation marks when the quoted words are a question.)

7. We toured the new facility; it is perfect for our office. (A semicolon is used between two complete sentences that are closely related and that are not separated by a coordinating conjunction, a subordinating conjunction, or a conjunctive adverb.)

8. Review the script this evening; we will discuss it at our morning meeting. (A semicolon is used between two complete sentences that are closely related and that are not separated by a coordinating conjunction, a subordinating conjunction, or a conjunctive adverb.)

9. David has examined our proposal; however, we are awaiting his comments. (Because this sentence is composed of two independent clauses joined by the conjunctive adverb *however*, a semicolon should precede the adverb.)

10. We wanted to vacation in Sydney; however, finances dictated that we vacation in Bethany Beach instead. (Correct: Because this sentence is composed of two independent clauses joined by the conjunctive adverb *however*, a semicolon should precede the adverb.)

11. Two years ago he promised to speak at this year's convention, but yesterday he changed his mind. (Because this sentence is composed of two independent clauses joined by the coordinating conjunction *but,* a comma should precede the conjunction, but no comma should follow the conjunction.)

12. The new driver sat tentatively behind the wheel of his mother's car, and his mother sighed deeply as her son turned on the ignition. (Because this

sentence is composed of two independent clauses joined by the coordinating conjunction *and,* a comma should precede the conjunction.)

13. As the sun set behind the gently rolling hills of Giverny, a rosy glow enveloped the tiny village. (Correct: When a dependent clause precedes an independent clause, the dependent clause at the beginning of the sentence should be followed by a comma.)

14. Although I enjoy traveling to new places on vacation, I am always glad to return home to familiar sights and sounds. (When a dependent clause precedes an independent clause, the dependent clause at the beginning of the sentence should be followed by a comma.)

15. I have just finished reading the short story "The Gift of the Magi." (A period should be placed inside a closing quotation mark.)

16. My neighbor said, "We need to do something about the deteriorating house across the street." (Correct: A period should be placed inside a closing quotation mark.)

17. The phrase "sizing up the opponent," often used in political contests, is actually a sports expression. (Correct: A comma should be placed inside a closing quotation mark.)

18. The first-prize poem, "My Homeland," was written by a recent Chinese immigrant. (A comma should be placed inside a closing quotation mark.)

19. a. We have completed our fiscal year budget report. (The enclosed executive summary is for your reference.) (The first word of a sentence that is not embedded in parentheses in another sentence should be capitalized, and the terminal punctuation should be placed inside the closing parenthesis.)

    b. We have completed our fiscal year budget report (the enclosed executive summary is for your reference). (The first word of a sentence that is embedded in parentheses in another sentence should not be capitalized, and the terminal punctuation should be placed outside the closing parenthesis.)

20. John will be able to purchase a new car if the car manufacturers implement their proposed rebates. (When a restrictive dependent clause follows an independent clause, no commas is used before the dependent clause.)

21. We plan to travel the entire distance to Vermont in one day unless we get too tired during the trip. (When a restrictive dependent clause follows an independent clause, no comma is used before the dependent clause.)

22. The Baltimore Orioles, who hope to make the playoffs, have acquired a new manager. (Because the clause *who hope to make the playoffs* is nonrestrictive, it should be set off with commas.)

23. We plan to move into the new headquarters building, which is in downtown Washington. (Because the clause *which is in downtown Washington* is nonrestrictive, it should be set off with commas.)

24. The girl who met us at the train station is my sister. (Because the clause *who met us at the train station* is restrictive, it should not be set off with commas.)

25. Peering at us from behind his wire-rimmed glasses, the desk clerk seemed to be sneering with contempt. (Correct: When a verbal phrase precedes an independent clause at the beginning of a sentence, the phrase should be followed by a comma.)

26. To finish the required work by Friday, we need to work late every night this week. (When a verbal phrase precedes an independent clause at the beginning of a sentence, the phrase should be followed by a comma.)

27. Taught by teachers without a college diploma, the children from the rural district could not compete academically with their suburban counterparts. (Correct: When a verbal phrase precedes an independent clause at the beginning of a sentence, the phrase should be followed by a comma.)

28. Erin, a brilliant young lady, was recently named one of 100 Presidential Scholars. (The nonrestrictive phrase *a brilliant young lady* should be set off with commas.)

29. Fair Oaks Mall, a large shopping complex in Northern Virginia, is in the midst of a major refurbishing. (The nonrestrictive phrase *a large shopping complex in Northern Virginia* should be set off with commas.)

30. We have received requests for information from IBM, Control Data, Sprint, and IconLogic. (No colon should follow the preposition *from* because the word group preceding the colon is not a complete sentence.)

31. Among the reports he has authored are *Tomorrow's Lakes and Rivers, Our Troubled Environment,* and *Improving Our Air*. (No colon should follow the verb *are* because the word group preceding the colon is not a complete sentence.)

32. The architect has designed the following buildings: the Airey Center in Cleveland, the Fitzpatrick Theater in Boston, and the Museum of the South in Atlanta. (Correct: The word *group* preceding the colon is a complete sentence. Remember that the word group following the colon does not have to be a complete sentence.)

33. He will be attending a 3-day conference in San Diego later this month. (A hyphen is used to connect *3* to *day* to indicate a unit modifier.)

34. We will use only fire-tested materials for upholstery in our buildings. (A hyphen is used to connect *fire* to *tested* to indicate a unit modifier.)

35. Government-owned property is exempt from the requirements of the new legislation. (A hyphen is used to connect *Government* to *owned* to indicate a unit modifier.)

36. Yours is on the table; ours is on the chair. (Correct: Possessive pronouns do not use apostrophes.)

37. I decided not to purchase the chair because its fabric is very delicate. (No apostrophe should be in the possessive pronoun *its*. The contraction *it's* is incorrect in this sentence.)

38. The book asks the central question, "Who is responsible for improving the economy in this country...?" (Correct: A question mark is placed inside the closing quotation mark when the quote is a question.)

39. On our trip we will visit London, England, June 5-10; Paris, France, June 10-15; Bern, Switzerland, June 15-18; and Munich, Germany, June 18-21. (When internal commas are used within one or more items in a series, each item in the series is followed by a semicolon.)

40. We have considered three different color schemes: mauve, gray, and white; green, rust, and beige; and green, salmon, and off-white. (When internal commas are used within one or more items in a series, each item in the series is followed by a semicolon.)

# Subject–Verb Agreement

1. Both the <u>instructor</u> and the <u>participant</u> *are* responsible for creating a positive climate for learning.

2. Every <u>editor</u> and <u>proofreader</u> *has* received a copy of the style manual.

3. Neither the donors nor the <u>recipients</u> *have* received invitations to the party.

4. Either expenditures or <u>revenue</u> *needs* to be adjusted.

5. A <u>group</u> of equations *is* included in the appendix.

6. <u>Mickey Manis</u>, as well as several other executives in the workshop, *feels* that this type of seminar is very valuable.

7. Gregory is one of the people <u>who</u> *have* been selected to attend the convention.

8. <u>Each</u> of the engineers *has* received a copy of the proposal.

9. <u>Some</u> (is, are) still here. *(Either verb is correct, depending on the antecedent to some.)*

10. <u>All</u> of the books were returned.

11. The final <u>analyses</u> are now complete.

12. The <u>criteria</u> for the selection have been determined.

13. <u>Ten months</u> is a long time to wait.

14. I just learned that <u>$15,000</u> *has* been donated anonymously.

15. There *are* the <u>materials</u> you requested.

16. Here *are* a <u>pen</u> and <u>piece</u> of paper.

17. <u>Most</u> of the letter *has* been typed.

18. Michael is one of the designers <u>who</u> *have* been selected for a special award.

19. <u>Neither</u> of the candidates *has* returned from lunch.

20. The <u>committee</u> *has* not yet completed its annual report.

21. The <u>manager</u>, along with his assistants, *is* attending the meeting.

22. <u>One</u> of the concerns expressed by our assistants *is* the need for additional software.

23. The <u>scissors</u> *are* on my desk.

24. <u>Fifty percent</u> of the cash *was* stolen from the cash register.

25. <u>Fifty percent</u> of the books *were* destroyed in the flood.

# Pronoun–Antecedent Agreement

Note: Other answers are possible.

1. a. The staff will start work on its new project next week.

   b. The staff will start work on their new projects next week.

2. The committee has not yet released its report. (Correct)

3. When the jury reaches a (its, the) verdict, the judge will inform us.

4. a. Someone who has developed a sensitivity to language will be very annoyed by grammar errors.

   b. If you have developed a sensitivity to language, you will be very annoyed by grammar errors.

5. Everyone has completed the course workshop assessment.

6. Someone has left a book in the classroom.

7. Everyone has a personal definition of "freedom."

8. A doctor should be responsive to the needs of patients.

9. a. If the findings are inconclusive, they will not persuade the jury.

   b. Inconclusive finds will not persuade the jury.

10. All employees will begin their vacations next Friday. (Correct)

11. a. Neither the players nor the coach has yet made a decision.

    b. Neither the players nor the coach has yet decided

12. a. My friend and adviser offered his suggestions. (Correct)

    b. My friend and adviser offered suggestions.

13. The managers and assistant managers must submit their reports by the first of the month. (Correct)

14. The cast will have a party after its final performance.

15. Workers at the concession area should count their money and turn in receipts at the end of each performance.

16. When seating patrons, an usher should smile.

17. Either the light technician or the prompter will give me a key.

18. No one can know if he/she will be promoted this year.

19. a. An elephant never eats a leaf or bark that has fungus growing on it.

    b. An elephant never eats a leaf or bark with fungus.

20. a. Neither of the two computers is known for its reliability.

    b. Neither of the two computers is known for reliability.

21. a. A family should install at least one carbon monoxide detector in the home.

    b. A family should install at least one carbon monoxide detector in its home.

22. a. Each staff member got a raise on the date of his/her anniversary with the agency.

    b. Staff members got a raises on the date of their anniversary with the agency.

23. The human resources department has changed the enrollment process for workshops.

24. a. When you have received a verbal reprimand from your supervisor, you should take it seriously.

    b. Those who have received a verbal reprimand from a supervisor should take it seriously.

25. a. The jury has rapidly completed deliberations.

    b. The jury has rapidly completed its deliberations.

    c. The jury has rapidly completed the deliberations.

# Pronoun Case

## *Nominative Pronouns and Objective Pronouns*

1. Either Barbara or *I* will handle this case. (Subjective case: *I* will handle this case.)

2. Brian and *I* have reviewed the data. (Subjective case: *I* have reviewed the data.)

3. It could have been *he* who called last night. (Subjective case: *He* could have been it.)

4. Was it Jennie or *he* who spoke at the conference? (Subjective case: *He* was it.)

5. The winner was *he* not Milton. (Subjective case: *He* was the winner.)

6. They promoted Lisa and *me* to supervisory positions. (Objective case: They promoted *me* to supervisory positions.)

7. The material was intended for Seth and *her*. (Objective case: The material was intended for *her*.)

## *Possessives, Contractions, and Comparisons*

1. That copy is *hers*. (Possessive pronouns do not use apostrophes.)

2. Juanita is a friend of *ours*. (Possessive pronouns do not use apostrophes.)

3. I understood *his* declining our offer. (A possessive pronoun is used before a gerund.)

4. We appreciate *your* reviewing the papers. (A possessive pronoun is used before a gerund.)

5. *Your* assertion is incorrect. (A possessive pronoun is used before a noun.)

6. *It's* inconceivable that the ruling could be overturned. (Contractions use apostrophes.)

7. Eva is brighter than *I*. (Use subjective case: Eva is brighter than *I am)*.

8. The joke offended Ethan more than *her*. (Use objective case: The joke offended Ethan more than *it offended her*.

9. The director is as concerned as *we*. (Use subjective case: The director is as concerned as *we are*.)

## *Appositives and Compounds*

1. Mr. Porter introduced the award-winning editors, Andy and *me*. (Objective case: Mr. Porter introduced *me*.)

2. The teacher expects *us* students to be perfect. (Objective case: The teacher expects *us* to be perfect.)

3. *We* students need to prepare carefully for class. (Subjective case: *We* need to prepare carefully for class.)

4. The copies are for George and *me*. (Objective case: The copies are for *me*.)

---

### Who, Whom, Etc.

1. They will hire *whoever* is best qualified for the position. (Subjective case: ...*he* is best qualified....)

2. The receptionist *whom* I upset has filed a grievance against me. (Objective case: ...I upset *him*....)

3. We need a manager *who* understands the difficulties of being a working mother in the middle of flu season. (Subjective case: ...*he* understands the difficulties....)

4. Linda is the account representative *whom* they were criticizing. (Objective case: ...they were criticizing *him*.)

5. Meryl, *whom* I consider to be a great homemaker, admits that she hates cooking and cleaning. (Objective case: ... I consider *him*....)

6. *Whose* book is this? (A possessive pronoun, not a contraction, is needed.)

# Pronoun Case Review

1. Marguerite has more education than *I*, but I am a more conscientious worker. (Subjective case: ...has more education than *I* do....)

2. Please send a brochure to Edward and *me*. (Objective case: ...*to me*.)

3. Julie is as sophisticated as *she*. (Subjective case: ...as *she*.)

4. Adam and *I* both attended last year's convention. (Subjective case: ...*I* attended....)

5. I suspect that it is *I*, not Terry, who will be expected to finish the project. (Subjective case: *I* am it.... Note: You have to change the verb form when you mentally reverse the sentence.)

6. The new representative is *she*, not James. (Subjective case: *She* is....)

7. I do not object to *your* going to the meeting. (Possessive Case: A possessive modifies a gerund.)

8. I appreciate *his* speaking before our group. (Possessive Case: A possessive modifies a gerund.)

9. I am pleased to introduce the chemist *whom* we all admire—Dr. Wang. (Objective case: ...we all admire *him*.)

10. The economist *who* visited our office may soon become a permanent member of the staff. (Subjective case: ...*he* visited....)

11. Clara, Carl, and *she* listened to the speaker. (Subjective case: ...*she* listened....)

12. Anna helped *them* with their work. (Objective case: Anna helped them....

13. *His* winning the Academy Award did not surprise the critics. (Possessive Case: A possessive modifies a gerund.)

14. Marilyn and *I* attended the luncheon. (Subjective case: ...*I* attended....)

15. The Senator arrived with Ms. McCoy and *him*. (Objective case: ...with *him*.

16. He was amazed by *your* arriving so early. (Possessive Case: A possessive modifies a gerund.)

17. They thought it was *she* who developed the film script. (Subjective case: ...*she* was it....)

18. The coach explained the rules to his son and *us*. (Objective case: ...to *us*.

19. That was an exciting proposal presented by Mrs. Phillips and *him*. (Objective case: ...by *him*.)

20. Bob and *she* derive great pleasure from vacationing at the beach. (Subjective case: *She* derives....)

21. Some veterinarians are better informed than *she*. (Subjective case: ...than *she* is.)

22. a. She helped you more than I. (Subjective case: ...than *I* did.)

    b. She helped you more than *me*. (Objective case: ...than she helped *me*.)

23. A year ago I went to a basketball game with Mitchell and *him*. (Objective case: ...with ...*him*.)

24. Mitchell and *he* idolize Michael Jordan. (Subjective case: ...*he* idolizes....)

25. *His* guarding the house helped the old woman. (Possessive Case: A possessive modifies a gerund.)

26. a. She seems to like Burton more than *me*. (Objective case: ...than she likes *me.)*

    b. She seems to like Burton more than *I*. (Subjective case: ...than I like *Burton.)*

27. It was *I* who voted for you as chairman. (Subjective case: *I* was it....)

28. The entry form from Mr. Pierce and *her* arrived today. (Objective case: ...from *her*....)

29. She is the person *who* arranged the party. (Subjective case: ...*he* arranged....)

30. We invited everyone *whom* you requested. (Objective case: ...you requested *him*.)

# Verb Tense and Mood

1. I always thought that Seattle, not Olympia, *is* the capital of Washington. (Use the present tense for a universal truth.)

2. I looked at the man warily, *checked* his identification, and then called the security desk for help. (Use verb tenses consistently in the same time frame: *looked*, *checked*, *called*.)

3. He was viewed as an authority on the subject because he *had studied* for four years at Harvard University. (Use the past perfect tense when one action happens before another action.)

4. I *have worked* at this company for 15 years, and I still enjoy my job here. (Use the present perfect tense to show an action that has started in the past and is still ongoing.)

5. According to the terms of your contract, you *shall* submit a weekly progress report. (Use *shall* for a mandatory action.)

6. Carla *has driven* me to work every day this week because my clutch *does* not *engage*. (Use the present perfect tense to show an action that has started in the past and is still ongoing.)

7. I recommend that Debby *be removed* from the committee. (Use the subjunctive mood in the dependent clause when the verb *recommend* is in the independent clause.)

8. Matthew demanded that Andrew *leave* the room at once. (Use the subjunctive mood in the dependent clause when the verb *demand* is in the independent clause.)

9. If I *were* your secretary, I would type the report for you. (Use the subjunctive mood in the dependent clause when the situation is contrary to fact.)

10. If I *am* appointed chairperson, I will change the meeting format. (Do not use the subjunctive mood in the dependent clause when the situation could occur.)

# Verb Forms

1. a. Frank *has gone* to work early every day this week.
   b. Frank *went* to work early every day this week.

2. a. I *have spoken* with my supervisor about the vacation schedule.
   b. I *spoke* with my supervisor about the vacation schedule.

3. A main water pipe *has sprung* a leak. (Correct)

4. I *rode* the bus to work today. (Correct)

5. I *have* never *broken* a promise to a friend. (Correct)

# Verb Tense

Note: Other answers are possible.

1.  I was surprised that the study said Washington *is* not our country's most important city. (Use the present tense for a universal truth.)

2.  He *walked* into the office and *started* to complain to me before he even said, "Good morning." (Use verb tenses consistently in the same time frame: *walked*, *started*.)

3.  I offered Ms. Lewis the job because she *has* already had 10 years of experience in our business. (Use the present perfect tense to show an action that has started in the past and is still ongoing.)

4.  By the time I arrived at the meeting, Kevin *had* already made his presentation. (Use the past perfect tense when one action happens before another action.)

5.  He spoke with the voice of experience because he *had* traveled extensively in Europe from 2009 until this year. (Use the past perfect tense when one action happens before another action.)

6.  The report *says* that cholesterol *is* a factor that *contributes* to heart disease. (Use the present tense for a universal truth.)

7.  The teacher told the class, "I *have* enjoyed working with you during the past 10 sessions." (Use the present perfect tense to show an action that has started in the past and is still ongoing.)

8.  I *have* performed at the Arena Stage for the past 10 years. (Use the present perfect tense to show an action that has started in the past and is still ongoing.)

9.  Ginny *has* arrived late to work every morning this week. (Use the present perfect tense to show an action that has started in the past and is still ongoing.)

10. The police officer told the driver to get out of the car, searched the car for drugs and weapons, and *said* nothing when he *discovered* a gun concealed under the front seat." (Use verb tenses consistently in the same time frame: *told, searched, said, discovered* or *tells, searches, says, discovers*.)

# Verb Mood

1. I recommend that she *be* appointed Director. (Use the subjunctive mood in the dependent clause when the verb *recommend* is in the independent clause.)

2. The President suggested that Chester *study* ways to improve the farm aid bill. (Use the subjunctive mood in the dependent clause when the verb *suggest* is in the independent clause.)

3. The Commission urged that Ms. Perez *reconsider* submitting her resignation. (Use the subjunctive mood in the dependent clause when the verb *urge* is in the independent clause.)

4. He insisted that Maria be removed from the room at once. (Use the subjunctive mood in the dependent clause when the verb *insist* is in the independent clause.)

5. If I were Chairman of the Federal Reserve Board, I would lower interest rates. (Use the subjunctive mood in the dependent clause when the situation is contrary to fact.)

6. If I were able to travel for free, I would roam around the world for the rest of my life. (Use the subjunctive mood in the dependent clause when the situation is contrary to fact.)

7. If he had been more attentive, he would have understood the directions. (Use the subjunctive mood in the dependent clause when the situation is contrary to fact. The dependent clause uses the past perfect to express past time when the clause is subjunctive.)

8. If she had been able to attend, she would have. (Use the subjunctive mood in the dependent clause when the situation is contrary to fact. The dependent clause uses the past perfect to express past time when the clause is subjunctive.)

9. If my associate had arrived at work on time, the report would have been typed by now. (Use the subjunctive mood in the dependent clause when the situation is contrary to fact. The dependent clause uses the past perfect to express past time when the clause is subjunctive.)

10. If we are able to resolve the problem, morale will improve. (Correct: Do not use the subjunctive mood in the dependent clause when the situation could occur.)

# Verb Tense

Note: Other answers are possible.

Pepper always *knew* precisely how to annoy someone. Pepper *was* a dog, a "regal" blend of Newfoundland and Australian Shepherd, two breeds that guarantee snobbery. This particular dog *knew* exactly when to come asking for food—just when the other dogs *had* already been fed and the food *had* been put away. He *understood* precisely when to want to go into a room—just when the door *had* been closed. He *was* uncanny at knowing exactly where to sit—right where I *wanted* to sweep the floor or, more unerringly annoying, right on the dirt I *had* already swept together. Pepper *knew* where to sit on a beautiful spring day—on the lounge chair (better known as his "throne") on the deck so no one else *could* enjoy the lovely weather. He *was* quite the social butterfly—whenever he *heard* the neighborhood dogs barking in "dogland," he *communicated* with them by bellowing his responses. He *had* the knack for perfect timing—as soon as I *snuggled* on the sofa with a good book and a steaming cup of tea, he *would come* behind me and *paw* the back of the sofa so I *would* get up and let him out. This dog *was* certainly the "perfect" dog.

# Parallelism

Note: Other answers are possible.

1. When touring other countries, he enjoyed eating the native food, visiting museums, and *walking* through the city. (Use parallel construction in a series: *eating, visiting, walking*.)

2. Her new job involves editing newsletter submissions, preparing copy for the printer, and *reviewing* page proofs prepared by the printer. (Use parallel construction in a series: editing, preparing, reviewing.)

3. He searched on the top of his cluttered desk, in the overcrowded bookshelves in his office, and through the stacks of papers under his desk. (Delete *he checked*. Use parallel construction in a series: on the..., in the..., through the....)

4. She enjoys reading and snowboarding. (Delete *the times of*. Use parallel construction with two coordinate items: *reading*, *snowboarding*)

5. a. He said that there will be promotion opportunities but that those promotions will be limited. (Use parallel construction with two dependent clauses.)

   b. He said there will be a limited number of promotions. (Eliminate the problem by using only one dependent clause.)

6. He must have *either forgotten our meeting or been caught* in traffic. (Use parallel construction with the correlative conjunction *either/or*.)

7. Cynthia has *neither the resources* to help pay for the party *nor the time* to help plan it. (Use parallel construction with the correlative conjunction *neither/nor*.)

8. Please follow this procedure:

   ❐ Reserve the room at least three weeks in advance.

   ❐ Send us list of the items you will need and a floor plan of the table and chairs.

   ❐ Arrive at least thirty minutes before the workshop begins to verify that the room is arranged as you requested. (Use parallel construction in a list.)

# Grammar Review

1. Either Mrs. Roth or her associates *have* edited the final draft. (Use the plural verb *have* to agree with the subject *associates*.)

2. Neither Barbara nor Gail *has* received the material. (Use the singular verb *has* to agree with the singular subject *Gail*.)

3. Mr. Abrams and *she* will attend the conference in Rome. (Correct: Use the subjective case for the subject: ...*she* will.... )

4. The company has invited Leah and *me* to participate in a panel discussion of editorial practices. (Use the objective case of the object of a verb: ...has invited...*me*....)

5. Neither of the plans *has* been approved by Mr. Andrews. (Use a singular verb when a singular pronoun is the subject: *Neither*...*has*....)

6. Either of the alternatives *is* an appropriate solution to our morale problem. (Correct: Use a singular verb when a singular pronoun is the subject: *Either*...*is*....)

7. One of the books *was* left in the auditorium. (Use a singular verb when a singular pronoun is the subject: *One*...*was*....)

8. Each of the invitations *is* embossed with a gold seal. (Correct: Use a singular verb when a singular pronoun is the subject: *Each*...*is*....)

9. a. There *are* many flights leaving for Boston from Dulles Airport. (Correct: When a subject follows the verb, be sure the subject and verb agree: *flights are*.)

   b. Many flights *are* leaving for Boston from Dulles Airport. (Rewrite the sentence to avoid the weak "There are...." structure.)

10. There *are* a package and a large envelope for you at the security desk. (When a subject follows the verb, be sure the subject and verb agree: *package* and *envelope are*.)

11. I insist that he *be* replaced as chairperson effective this Friday. (Use the subjunctive mood in the dependent clause when the verb *insist* is in the independent clause.)

12. I move that $200 *be* appropriated to purchase a scanner. (Use the subjunctive mood in the dependent clause when the verb *move* is in the independent clause.)

13. If he *were* able to speak to the convention, he would do so. (Use the subjunctive mood in the dependent clause when the situation is contrary to fact.)

14. If he *is* able to speak to the convention, he will do so. (Correct: Do not use the subjunctive mood in the dependent clause when the situation could occur.)

15. The phenomena *have* been observed by many astronomers. (Use a plural verb with a plural subject: *phenomena have*. Use a singular verb with a singular subject: *phenomenon has*.)

16. The data *have* been analyzed by our scientists. (Correct: Use a plural verb with a plural subject: *data have*. Use a singular verb with a singular subject: *datum has*.)

17. a. Anybody who is available to help with registration should contact *a* local representative. (Use a singular article [*a*] with a singular indefinite pronoun: The pronoun *their* is plural; the pronoun *anybody* is singular.)

    b. Those who are available to help with registration should contact *their* local representative. (Recast the sentence in the plural. The pronoun *their* is plural; the pronoun *those* is plural.)

18. Everybody has a right to express *an opinion* on the issues. (Do not use a plural pronoun to refer to a singular indefinite pronoun. The pronoun *their* is plural; the pronoun *everybody* is singular.)

19. Our new neighbor is as friendly as *he*. (Subjective case: ...as *he* is.)

20. The reorganization has affected Michael more than *me*. (Objective case: ...than it has affected *me*.)

21. She *herself* would never attempt such a risky venture. (Correct: Use the reflexive pronoun for emphasis.)

22. Please send the original pictures and the negatives to Austin and *me*. (Objective case: ...to *me*.)

23. We have sent a brochure to *whoever* requested one. (Subjective case: ...*he* requested one.)

24. I would like to introduce Charles Monihan, *whom* we recently selected to serve as office manager. (Objective case: ...selected *him*....)

25. I have discussed the problem with my staff, and they *agree* that we must improve our response time to member queries. (Use present tense for an action happening in the present.)

26. The PTA lobbies for the educational needs of children, supports teachers in the public schools, and *expresses* high expectations for the products of American classrooms. (Use verb tenses consistently in the same time frame: *lobbies*, *supports*, *expresses*.)

27. The soccer team has won all of *its* Division 2 games this fall. (Use a singular pronoun to agree with the singular antecedent: *its, team*.)

28. a. The group *have* reached their individual goals for this year. (Correct: The collective noun *group* has a plural concept. Use the plural pronoun *their*.)

    b. The group members have reached their individual goals for this year. (Recast the sentence.)

29. The winner of the annual All-Around Achiever Award is *she*, not Josh, the expected winner. (Correct: Subjective case: *She* was the winner...)

30. a. It is *they* who will be held accountable for the problems. (Correct: Subjective case: *They* are...)

    b. They are the ones who will be held responsible. (Recast the sentence.)

31. She is the *faster* of the two sisters. (Correct: Use the ending *-er* when comparing two things or people)

32. The defense attorney presented a strong case for his client, but the case presented by the prosecution was the *stronger*. (Use the ending *-er* when comparing two things or people)

33. He moved so *quickly* that he disappeared from the room before I had an opportunity to acknowledge his presence. (Use an adverb to modify a verb.)

34. In public he spoke as *smoothly* as a politician, but in private he was shy and taciturn. (Use an adverb to modify a verb.)

35. I recently learned that English *is* actually a Germanic language. (Use the present tense for a universal truth.)

36. The report *says* that potatoes *are* not fattening. (Use the present tense for a universal truth.)

37. Every manager will receive *a* copy of the revised manual by Monday. (Avoid sexist language.)

38. A doctor must strive to meet the needs of patients. (Delete *his* to avoid sexist language.)

39. The association will hold *its* (or *the*) annual convention in Hawaii this winter. (Use a singular pronoun or a definite article when the antecedent is singular: its or the, association.)

40. The corporation has informed *its* stockholders that there will be no dividend this quarter. (Use a singular pronoun when the antecedent is singular: *its*, *corporation*.)

41. The vice president of investments assessed the daily market fluctuations. (Change passive voice to active voice.)

42. While the mechanic was fixing the flat tire, the lug wrench broke in his hand. (Correct the dangling modifier. The wrench cannot fix the flat tire.)

43. Ms. Oliver is the specialist who *is* assigned to write the proposal. (Correct: The antecedent to *who* is *specialist*, which is singular.)

44. Ms. Oliver is one of the specialists who *are* assigned to write the proposal. (The antecedent to *who* is *specialists*, which is plural.)

45. Ms. Oliver is the only one of the specialists who *is* assigned to write the proposal. (Correct: The antecedent to *who* is *only one*, which is singular.)

46. The young senator tends to vote *conservatively*. (Use an adverb to modify a verb.)

## Notes

# Index

CPSIA information can be obtained
at www.ICGtesting.com
Printed in the USA
LVHW01s1429270918
591585LV00006B/288/P

9 781944 607210